ALISTER MACKENZIE'S MASTERPIECE

The Augusta National Golf Club

Stan Byrdy

Stan Byrdy

Illustrations by William Lanier III

An imprint of Augusta Golf Tours, LLC
All inquiries should be addressed to:
Stan Byrdy stan.byrdy@gmail.com

Printed and bound in the United States.

09   08   07   06   05   1   2   3   4   5

Library of Congress Cataloging-in-Publication Data

Byrdy, Stan, 1953-
The Augusta National Golf Club : Alister MacKenzie's masterpiece / Stan Byrdy. p. cm.
Includes bibliographical references.
ISBN 978-0-692-84816-6
1. Augusta National Golf Club. 2. Golf courses--Design and construction.
I. Mackenzie, A. (Alexander), b. 1870. II. Title.

GV969.A83B97 2005
796.352'06'075864--dc22
2004027003

Book and jacket design by Somberg Design
www.sombergdesign.com

Dedicated to

My friend, my hero, my dad,

Stanley W. Byrdy

The Byrdy family of Youngstown, Ohio

And to my loving wife, Donna, and newborn son,

David, for their support and inspiration during

the research, writing, and production

of this project.

Contents

The Starter

Minding MacKenzie

Born Alexander MacKenzie in Normanton, York, England, on the next to last day of August 1870, Alister, as he was known, was equally proud of his father's Scottish roots. Following graduation from Cambridge University, where he obtained degrees in medicine, chemistry, and natural science, MacKenzie practiced medicine alongside his father in the town of Leeds.

But young MacKenzie secretly harbored other interests that ironically began to take shape with the outbreak of the Boer War. The conflict between Britain and the two Boer Republics was staged in South Africa at the turn of the nineteenth century. Outnumbered nearly ten to one, the Boers utilized guerrilla tactics to perfection in staving off the British from October 1899 to May 1902. Serving as a field surgeon in the British Army, MacKenzie got a firsthand view of the Boers' tactic of camouflaging their troops in the field. MacKenzie would soon use this same technique in the design of golf courses.

At the conclusion of the Boer conflict, MacKenzie headed back to England and resumed his work in medicine. But a lukewarm interest for the profession eventually gave way to his ultimate calling in life, of which he was most passionate. His artistic flair and surgeon's touch came in handy in his new career as a golf course architect. Coupled with a camouflage expert's eye for detail and an innate feel for the land, MacKenzie was blessed with a unique but practical design perspective.

His ability to showcase nuances that others neither saw nor were remotely aware of and his knack of utilizing so little to accomplish much were considered revolutionary. Even MacKenzie's own club at Leeds refused to adopt his philosophies on the grounds that the ideas were far too radical. His view of designing inland layouts to resemble the far superior seaside links courses of the day was a new concept. MacKenzie's ideas for better utilizing the natural lay of the land and camouflaging artificial hazards were hard for golf committees of his day to grasp let alone accept. It only made sense then, as now, that the more money spent on a project the better it must be.

In a day of increased specialization, MacKenzie found it puzzling that committees comprised of specialists in their respective fields of medicine, law, and engineering held such little regard for a skilled golf course architects. But most committees of the time hesitated to hire noted design artists for fear it would be an expensive exercise. A proponent of cost-efficient courses with more mental than manual labor, MacKenzie's designs featured fewer bunkers and more strategy. His wide, undulating layouts proved friendly to beginners and challenging to professionals. MacKenzie noted that many committees were more than willing to pay great amounts of capital for manual labor, but not for the necessary mental labor that gave the course its heart and soul. The end results, in MacKenzie's view, were inferior artificial courses that cost twice as much to produce.

MacKenzie was also convinced that most golfers believed they were capable of course design and professional golfers proved especially annoying to him: "I remarked before, that although I know scores of excellent golf courses designed by amateur golfers, I did not know of a single outstanding one by a professional golfer. Not that there are not plenty of professionals who are men of considerable education, but the fact that they are constantly playing competitive golf makes them view with resentment anything that is likely to disturb their sequence of threes and fours."

In 1905, when MacKenzie and associates put in motion the plan to form Alwoodley Golf Club, his design plans were again rejected. Committee meetings grew so heated that according to MacKenzie, "on many an occasion we nearly came to blows." MacKenzie's "less is more" philosophy ran head-on into the "glitz over substance" thinking of his day. It was only when noted designer Harry S. Colt agreed to intervene and approved of MacKenzie's work that the committee at Alwoodley would even consider his plans. But no sooner than Colt was out of sight than MacKenzie's work was out of mind.

Undeterred, MacKenzie caught a much welcome break when an unusually rough winter settled over England. A majority of the new club's committee members stayed away from the site during the harsh weather and MacKenzie and an associate took a free reign at designing the course as they pleased. Come spring when the full compliment of committee members toured the site, according to MacKenzie some grew so enraged at what they saw that "once more we nearly came to blows." In an effort to keep peace within the club, it was agreed that the layout would be played as it was for the upcoming season and changes administered the following winter. Being a diplomat first and artist second was how Alister MacKenzie got his start. As it turned out, no major changes were ever made to his design at Alwoodley. It was the first of approximately 150 (though MacKenzie reported the number to be over 400) courses throughout the world that would eventually bear MacKenzie's mark.

Armed with newfound confidence in his design abilities, in 1909 MacKenzie set his sights next on the layout at neighboring Moortown, a patch of land that closely resembled the moorland property at Alwoodley. With only $500 in funds with which to work, MacKenzie spent all the money on the design of one great hole that came to be known as the Gibraltar Hole.

The impressively designed hole served as a showpiece for prospective members and helped raise the funds necessary to finish the layout. The design proved so unique that two decades later Moortown Golf Club was chosen to host the first Ryder Cup Matches in England.

As his design career seemed destined to go forward, there would be one more stint in the British armed forces before embarking on his life's work. With the outbreak of World War I, MacKenzie convinced the British that his talents would best be served in an area other than medicine and he was soon sent to head up a school of camouflage at Hyde Park in London.

At the war's conclusion MacKenzie devoted his pursuits to golf design full time and penned his book, *Golf Architecture*. Excerpts of his thirteen "essential features of an ideal course" are featured in "MacKenzie's Magic." Shortly thereafter, he headed for the United States where golf was taking the country by storm and where he could further his skills working alongside noted architects such as Perry Maxwell.

In two books penned by MacKenzie, the aforementioned *Golf Architecture*, published in 1920, and The *Spirit of St. Andrews*, printed for the first time in 1995, the influence of his military career on later design work is painfully evident. The influence of two wars on MacKenzie was lasting and careers as camouflage artist and course designer were likely blurred so as to become inseparable. MacKenzie's genius lay in a unique perspective honed from a skill-set different from any course architect in history.

"I am sitting in my veranda at the present moment on the edge of the sixth fairway of the Pasatiempo Course," the sixty-two-year-old MacKenzie wrote in *The Spirit of St. Andrews*. "I have just remarked to my wife that there are two bunkers within a hundred yards of her capable of concealing a hundred soldiers in each and machine guns in a defensive position." The passage is a telling reminder of how MacKenzie's past was part of his long held view of strategic course design.

According to MacKenzie, "There is a marked

MacKenzie concluded, "In golf architecture and camouflage a knowledge of psychology is of enormous value..."

similarity in the mentality between the regular soldier and the professional golfer." Likewise in MacKenzie's eyes, "There are many other attributes in common between the successful golf architect and the camoufleur. Both, if not actually artists, must have had an artistic temperament, and have had an education in science. Surprise is the most important thing in war, and by camouflage you are able to obtain this not only on the defense but in the attack."

MacKenzie concluded, "In golf architecture and camouflage a knowledge of psychology is of enormous value. It enables one to judge what is likely to give pleasurable excitement to the golfer and confidence and improvement in morale to the soldier. The writer feels most strongly that his experience in the Great War [World War I] in visualizing and surveying miles of sites for fortifications in this country and abroad, in map-reading, in the interpretation of aerial photography, in drainage and labor-saving problems, and particularly in the mental training of strategic camouflage and devising traps and surprises to the enemy, was by no means wasted even from a golf-course point of view."

In late 1926, while Donald Ross was busy on his new design at Forest Hills in Augusta, Georgia, and shortly thereafter the major redesign at Augusta Country Club, MacKenzie was working on a layout with Alex Russell at Australia's Royal Melbourne West Course. This intriguing design posed as much mental as physical challenge to golfers and brought Alister MacKenzie's name to the forefront of golf course

architecture. The Royal Melbourne West design would prove to be the first of many jewels in MacKenzie's brilliant career and is widely regarded as the best golf course south of the equator.

The late 1920s proved important to MacKenzie on several other counts. What would be hailed as two more jewels in his career, Cypress Point and Pasatiempo, were being completed along California's Monterey Bay. MacKenzie filed divorce papers in 1929 from his first wife Edith Wedderburn in England and the following year married a widow, Hilda Haddock, in California. It was in the midst of this emotional time in MacKenzie's life that he was reacquainted with Bobby Jones. Their chance meeting in the fall of 1929 in California set in motion the design of the future Augusta National Golf Club.

It was during the week of the 1929 U.S. Amateur at Pebble Beach that MacKenzie's West Coast designs came to the attention of Bobby Jones. Prior to the start of the Amateur, Jones had the opportunity to play the Cypress Point layout along the Monterey Peninsula and was smitten by its well-thought-out design and natural beauty. Jones was particularly impressed with the well-devised landing areas, which MacKenzie set in place with the help of a young golfer named Lewis Lapham. The son of one of Cypress Point's charter members, young Lapham smashed golf shots alongside MacKenzie to best determine the "heroic carry" of its holes. All the while, MacKenzie plotted the layout and landing areas and incorporated his well-honed

MacKenzie's thirteen rules of design served as his badge of honor and were closely aligned with Jones' design philosophies.

camouflage techniques into the design. It was an idea not lost on Bobby Jones and one he would soon imitate in the design of his dream course in Augusta.

In competition at the 1929 U.S. Amateur, Jones posted 145 during medal play, good for cohonors, and seemed assured of waltzing to another major championship. But in the first round of match-play competition, this golf legend with nine majors to his credit was beaten 1-up by relatively unknown Johnny Goodman. Though he had unofficially bested Goodman by one shot overall on the scorecard, Jones was eliminated from the tournament. While his defeat stunned the golf world, it proved fortuitous for the sport on a much larger scale.

With time to spare before heading home to Georgia, Jones accepted an invitation from 1921 U.S. Women's Amateur champion Marion Hollins to play her new course and yet another MacKenzie design, Pasatiempo. MacKenzie tagged along as Jones played golf and the duo shared ideas on a passion they both entertained, the design and construction of golf courses.

Jones was no doubt aware of MacKenzie's work, at least in theory. In 1927 he had received a signed copy of MacKenzie's first book, *Golf Architecture*, but now the proof was in front of him. The ability to view MacKenzie's artistry firsthand and speak with him in person lent credence to this meeting that soon proved a blessing for each. Pasatiempo provided the backdrop and nearby Cypress Point a reference point for this meeting of the minds.

MacKenzie's thirteen rules of design served as his badge of honor and were closely aligned with Jones' design philosophies. Jones especially liked MacKenzie's ideas of a wide open course that featured fewer bunkers, more undulations, and provided enjoyment to golfers of all skill levels. Most of all, the two shared a deep respect for the Old Course at St. Andrews and agreed that the seaside links layout in Scotland was the best in the world. MacKenzie noted in his book *The Spirit of St. Andrews*, "I believe that the real reason St. Andrews' Old Course is infinitely superior to anything else is owing to the fact that it was constructed when no one knew anything about the subject at all, and since then it has been considered too sacred to be touched."

MacKenzie deemed a good golf course to be similar to a work of art, like a treasure created by a sculptor, composer, or other such skilled professional whose work can only be fully appreciated over time. He reasoned that "A good golf course is like good music or good anything else; it is not necessarily a course which appeals the first time one plays over it, but which grows on the player the more frequently he visits it." The message struck a chord with Bobby Jones, an artist in his own right, whose Jekyll and Hyde experiences at St. Andrews had exposed the best and worst in his game and character.

Early in his career, the temperamental Jones felt the many natural features of the course and its countless undulations, swales, and bunkers to be unfair. At age nineteen and on his first trip to St. Andrews for the 1921 British Open, Jones suffered his "most inglorious failure in golf." After a front-nine 46 during third-round play, Jones' efforts only got worse. The nineteen-year-old Jones posted a double-bogey six at the tenth hole and then, while mired in Hell bunker at the eleventh hole, he picked up his golf ball and walked off the course. But as his golf game evolved so did his perspective. It was only when his game and viewpoints matured that Jones came to recognize the nuances at St. Andrews for their intended strategic value. It was the seaside links at St. Andrews that were far superior to any inland course and represented the ultimate design challenge.

In The *Spirit of St. Andrews*, Bobby Jones wrote in the foreword of MacKenzie's book, "Like myself, Dr. MacKenzie is a lover of old St. Andrews. Of course, like everyone else, he despairs of ever producing anything quite so good, but the doctor's experience with camouflage and his innate artistry enable him to convert an inland terrain into something surprisingly like the seaside links land, which is the very best golfing country." What MacKenzie and Jones despaired, they later created over 365 acres of property in Augusta, Georgia.

At the time of their West Coast meeting, Jones was just twenty-seven years of age, and MacKenzie fifty-nine. Despite the difference in age, the two were singular in mind on the subject of golf course design. Jones came away from the meeting impressed that he had found the artist capable of sculpting an inland course with seaside features similar to those at St. Andrews.

There was one small matter of business that needed attending to first. With each successful step of Jones' journey toward the Grand Slam, his future dream golf course came that much closer to reality. In the summer of 1930, Jones accomplished the feat that no golfer before or since has been able to deliver in one season, the "impregnable quadrilateral" of golf. With the Grand Slam achieved, another piece of the puzzle that would become MacKenzie's masterpiece fell neatly into place.

The Manor The future clubhouse of the Augusta National Golf Club was known as "the Manor" when it was the residence of the Berckmans family, who owned and operated Fruitlands Nurseries on the grounds from the mid 1800s to the early twentieth century. The now-famous structure and nurseries offices building (foreground) are covered here with a rare dusting of snow. (© Historic Golf Prints – Ron Watts Collection.)

Creating the Canvas

Spanish explorer Hernando de Soto was reported to have traveled across the property in his search for gold in the mid-1500s (slivers of gold were later found on the property), and General James Edward Oglethorpe was said to have met with Indians on the land in the early 1730s. During Revolutionary War times, a tavern was situated near the entrance to Magnolia Lane, and by the mid-1800s an indigo plantation covered the acreage. In 1857 the property was purchased by a noted horticulturalist who started a nursery. In the early 1900s the property was the prized site of a proposed winter resort and, finally, Bobby Jones' dream golf course. The land on which the Augusta National Golf Club is located has played a major role in the town's storied history, though no one could possibly foresee the events that would transform this small plot of land into the most revered golf course in the world.

An outpost along the Savannah River, Augusta emerged as a gateway to the west and during the Revolutionary War the state capital was relocated here. In 1789 the Constitution of the United States was ratified by the state of Georgia in Augusta. With equal parts hard work, sheer coincidence, and blessings from a higher power, the stepping stones to the Augusta National Golf Club began to fall in place as far back as 1854. It was then, on the site of his indigo plantation, that Dennis Redmond constructed the first home in the South made of concrete. A century and a half later, at the end of a long entrance lined with magnolia trees, the structure serves today as the clubhouse of the Augusta National Golf Club.

In 1857 Redmond's failed indigo plantation was purchased by Louis Mathieu Edouard Berckmans, a Belgian baron more commonly referred to in Augusta as Baron Berckmans. The baron and horticulturalist son Prosper Julius Alphonse viewed the land as a business opportunity and formed the Fruitlands Nurseries, the largest enterprise of its kind in the South. The company imported trees and plants from the far reaches of the earth and developed the business into a commercial success. In the late 1850s the Berckmans planted sixty-one magnolia trees along the entrance lane to their residence known affectionately as "the Manor." Before Baron Berckmans died in 1893 and son Prosper in 1910, they witnessed what would prove to be a foretelling event in their property's and the city of Augusta's history.

Prior to the Civil War, Augusta developed its canal to bolster industry. Spared the onslaught of Sherman's Army in his march to the sea, Augusta prospered as much of the South slowly rebuilt from the ashes at war's end. The twenty-five years immediately following the Civil War proved heady times of wealth and expansion in Augusta. During Reconstruction, Augusta was widely viewed as the model city of the South. To mark the quarter-century of unparalleled prosperity and the one hundred years since the signing of the U.S. Constitution in Augusta, city fathers decided a celebration was in order. Prosper Berckmans helped head up the early charge for the event, which eventually caught the fancy of the nation and came to be known as the Augusta National Exposition of 1888, the city's first "Augusta National." Ironically, just shy of a half-century later Berckmans' own property would come to bear that name.

It was the Augusta National Exposition of 1888 that

Snow Magnolia, circa 1895 Snowfall covers the entrance to Magnolia Lane in the late 1800s. (Courtesy of Augusta Museum of History.)

fanned the flames for Augusta's transition from industrial might to winter resort and golf town. One of the largest fairs ever to take place in the South, the six-week-long exposition attracted wealthy industrialists looking to showcase their wares. An expo center on the scale of a large shopping mall was constructed, the grand Bon Air Hotel was rushed to completion, and Augusta welcomed the world. When visitors glimpsed Augusta's wide and lighted boulevards and experienced firsthand its southern charm and moderate late-fall weather, a new era in the city's history began.

By the time of Baron Berckmans' death in 1893, Augusta's role as a winter destination point had been established. When son Prosper passed away in 1910, the exclusive winter resort and golf facilities flourished at his doorstep. The Berckmans' home at the end of the magnolia-lined lane was conveniently located in the midst of Augusta's resort expansion. From the cupola of the Manor facing east, the Berckmans' could surely see the lights of the mighty Hampton Terrace Hotel across the Savannah River in North Augusta, South Carolina. The grand hotel was the largest wooden structure on the face of the earth when it debuted in 1903.

Just eighteen miles farther east sat the proud community of Aiken, South Carolina, and its prize winter resorts. Aiken is home to the Palmetto Golf Club, the first golf course in the southeastern United States, and the layout Alister MacKenzie redesigned after finishing his work at the Augusta National. Just to the west of the Berckmans' property lay the Augusta Country Club in the ritzy Summerville District, with its bustling Hill area, Bon Air Hotel , and Partridge Inn. By then, the Bon Air's original golf course had grown into the Lake Course and the Augusta Country Club was in the process of adding its Hill Course.

After his death in 1910, Prosper Berckmans' widow inherited the property. Berckmans' young widow and sons remained divided over the operation of Fruitlands Nurseries and its 365 acres of prize property. In the midst of Augusta's rise as the nation's top winter tourism destination site, the prize property was sold off. Two of Prosper Berckmans' three sons, Louis Alphonse and Prosper Julius Alphonse, later reentered the picture to work with Alister MacKenzie and Bobby Jones.

When the Hampton Terrace Hotel was lost to fire on New Years' Eve 1916, Augusta's winter resort and golf industry was dealt a severe setback. The need for additional resort space fell back to the Augusta side of the Savannah River, where the chic Bon Air Hotel and

Berckmans Bunch, circa 1890 Belgian Baron Louis Mathieu Edouard Berckmans and family at home in Augusta. Berckmans purchased the property and began operating the Fruitlands Nurseries in 1858 on the land where the Augusta National Golf Club is now located. (© Historic Golf Photos–Ron Watts Collection.)

Growing Tall, circa 1890s Trees being grown on the grounds of the Fruitlands Nurseries. (© Historic Golf Photos–Ron Watts Collection.)

Bon Air Vanderbilt, circa 1930 When the original wooden Bon Air Hotel burned in 1921, the structure was replaced with a new cement structure. The Bon Air Vanderbilt accommodated guests for the three-day grand opening of the Augusta National Golf Club in January 1933. (Courtesy of Joseph M. Lee III.)

Partridge Inn were forced to turn winter guests away. As it was, the cozy Partridge Inn expanded on a year to year basis and grew from a quaint lodging house to elegant resort hotel. Just five years after the Hampton Terrace burned, the Bon Air Hotel on "The Hill" in Augusta suffered the same fate. Now the two grand hotels that once overlooked downtown Augusta from both sides of the Savannah River were gone. In their brief histories the grand hotels had hosted the elite of American society. Presidents William H. Taft and Warren G. Harding had vacationed at the Bon Air and baseball great Ty Cobb resided nearby. John D. Rockefeller wintered at each of the grand hotels. Heads of state and industry, university presidents, noted politicians, military leaders, medical minds, actors, athletes, and accomplished artists in all fields rubbed shoulders in Augusta.

It was only a matter of time before other resort hotels replaced the grand facilities that had burned. The Bon Air Hotel was rebuilt of a concrete substance and reopened in 1923 as the Bon Air Vanderbilt. Smaller in dimension, the new hotel was as grand as the structure it replaced and later served as host for the Augusta National's official opening celebration in 1933. In the meantime, the construction of two more winter resorts that figured prominently into Bobby Jones' future was announced.

Two new developments were made public in 1925, in the midst of the Roaring Twenties, when Augusta's fame as a winter resort reached its zenith. First was the Forest Hills Ricker Hotel and Golf Course, which went from World War I army camp to grand resort in less than ten years. Opened in 1926, the Ricker Hotel was

Expo Center, circa 1888 Site of the Augusta National Exposition that helped transform the city into a winter tourism site. (Courtesy of Augusta Museum of History.)

equal to the grand winter resorts of Augusta's past. Donald Ross designed the hotel's golf course complete with the first grass greens in Augusta. It was here that Bobby Jones concluded the final two rounds of the 1930 Southeastern Open against an international field. His thirteen-shot margin of victory provided Jones with the vision that would sustain him in his bid for the Grand Slam.

Late in 1925, the announcement of yet another grand resort captured Augusta's attention and, later,

Bobby Jones' heart. The October 1, 1925, edition of the *Augusta Chronicle* blared across its front page in large, bold print, "Augusta Secures Fleetwood Hotel." A photo of the proposed fifteen-story high-rise hotel was included with the proclamation that "Commodore Stoltz Announces Plans for Two Million Dollar Hostelry on Berckmans Tract. On the site of 'The Manor,' quaint and delightful old home of the late P. J. A. Berckmans, nestled back of two rows of beautiful magnolia trees, the Fleetwood of Augusta will be built."

Partridge Putting, circa 1916 On cold winter nights the lobby of the Partridge Inn was converted into a putting surface and grew to be a popular tourist attraction. (Courtesy of Augusta Museum of History.)

The resort complex was the vision of Commodore J. Perry Stoltz, who planned to pattern the facility after his magnificent Fleetwood Hotel and broadcast center then in operation in Miami, Florida. One of several sites throughout the south that Stoltz was in the process of securing, Augusta would serve as a key link between New York and Miami.

The proposed 300-room facility was slated to be fifteen stories high, with a broadcast tower extending its reach another 100 feet. Had it been constructed it would have been the tallest structure in Augusta to this day. The top floor of the proposed hotel was to house a broadcast radio station and concert studio, complete with an express elevator from the ground floor. A dining room and kitchen area would occupy the floor immediately below.

The ground floor of the hotel was reserved for a series of boutiques, laundry, and ice and refrigeration equipment. Along the length of the entire first floor a large veranda was to be constructed. The next twelve stories were planned with rooms for winter guests and built in such a way that the entire structure faced the once famous nursery, on which was planned a championship eighteen-hole golf course.

The Fleetwood Hotel and golf facility were scheduled to be ready by New Years' Day, 1927. According to reports in the Augusta Chronicle, Stanley Wright was Stoltz's chief engineer for the project and would also make plans for construction of the golf course. Stoltz's original vision for the Fruitland Nurseries as an international resort, golf course, and broadcast center was not far from the one later realized by Bobby Jones.

With concrete footings for the resort poured, Stoltz's dream for Augusta was derailed in September when the Great Hurricane of 1926 hit Miami and wiped out his fortune.

In January 1926, Wright began to stake out the Fleetwood's foundation and design its golf course. The grand hotel was planned to sit just south of the Fruitlands Manor (the present Augusta National Clubhouse), "and it will not be necessary to tear down this quaint old structure for some time after the hotel is started." Stolz planned to utilize the quaint manor as temporary office space during construction of the resort hotel, then level the structure.

With concrete footings for the resort poured, Stoltz's dream for Augusta was derailed in September when the Great Hurricane of 1926 hit Miami and wiped out his fortune. The Category 4 hurricane ravaged downtown Miami and wreaked havoc on Stoltz's Miami Fleetwood Hotel and expansion plans. In the wake of the major hurricane, Stoltz filed for bankruptcy and the prize property along Washington Road in Augusta again lay dormant. Bad luck for Stoltz proved fortunate for Bobby Jones and the golf world. Five years later, Jones happened across Stoltz's early construction efforts when he announced a new vision for the property. Like Stoltz before him, Jones faced major hurdles in accomplishing his dream but, unlike Stoltz, he eventually cleared them.

Brilliant Brushstrokes

With nine major victories already on his résumé, Bobby Jones began the historic Grand Slam season of 1930 with a second-place finish in the Savannah Open in late February. Though he set the course single-round scoring record twice in four rounds, he finished one shot in back of eventual winner Horton Smith. One month later, Jones took part in the Southeastern Open in Augusta, an event staged over two Donald Ross designs, the Augusta Country Club and the Ricker Hotel's Forest Hills Golf Course. An international field was assembled that included three future Masters champions: Horton Smith, 1934 and 1936; Gene Sarazen,1935; and Henry Picard,1938. Jones responded with the tournament of a lifetime and provided a glimpse of the historic summer to follow.

To be fair, Jones was an honorary member of the Augusta Country Club and knew the design well. A last-minute entry, Smith had to be coaxed into the field by organizers, and only on the condition that he be flown immediately afterward to a previously scheduled engagement. Smith was accommodated with an early tee time on the final day of the event and an awaiting flight from nearby Daniel Field at the end of his round. Though he arrived late for the tournament in Augusta and did not get in a practice round on two courses he had never seen, it likely would not have mattered. The performance Jones rendered served notice that 1930 would be an unprecedented year in golf history.

The first two rounds of the tournament were scheduled for Monday, March 31, at the Augusta Country Club. Jones posted rounds of 72-72 over the tough Hill Course to take a three-shot lead after the opening day's play. Johnny Ferrell, who defeated Jones in a playoff

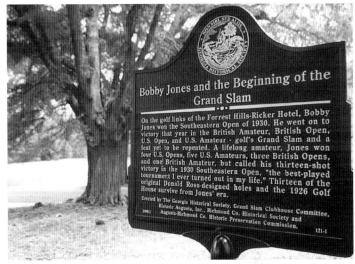

Forest Hills Marker Marker commemorating Bobby Jones' runaway victory in the 1930 Southeastern Open that provided him the Grand Slam vision. (Courtesy of Forest Hills Golf Club.)

two years earlier for the U.S. Open title, was one of two golfers in second place. Horton Smith was all alone in fourth place at four over par at the halfway point.

The final two rounds at Forest Hills Golf Course the following day only served to punctuate Jones' domination. Jones played the par-71 course two shots under par for an overall total of 284 for the tournament. Though he played the final three holes at four over par, Jones still managed to win the event by thirteen shots. Horton Smith finished eleven shots over par to pocket the first place money of $1,000 as top professional in the field. Playing alongside Horton that day was Ed

Southeastern Success circa 1930 A large gallery was on hand to witness Bobby Jones compete in the final two rounds of the 1930 Southeastern Open at Forest Hills Golf Club. Jones won the event by 13 shots over runner-up Horton Smith. The victory set the stage for Jones' quest to win the Grand Slam that summer. (Courtesy Joseph M. Lee III.)

Dudley, who established a new course record of 65 in the third round. Dudley finished one shot in back of Smith, good for $750, and would later become Jones' handpicked first head professional at the Augusta National.

Though he could not accept prize money as an amateur, Jones had the victory that gave substance to his dream. That summer he won the British Amateur at St. Andrews, the British Open at Hoylake, and followed with wins in the U.S. Open at Interlachen and the U.S. Amateur at Merion to complete his Grand Slam journey. Among all these tournaments it was the Southeastern Open that fueled his imagination and Jones later ranked his performance in Augusta as the best competitive golf of his career.

In the closing moments of the Southeastern Open, golfer Bobby Cruickshank turned to sportswriter O. B. Keeler and made this prophetic observation about Jones: "He'll go over to Britain and win the Open and the Amateur, and then he'll come back to America and win the open and the amateur—that's all he'll do this year." Cruickshank, who lost to Jones seven years earlier in a playoff for the U.S. Open, had seen all he needed to. After the lopsided event in Augusta, he reportedly wagered the sizeable amount of $500 in Great Britain on Jones to win the Grand Slam. Bookmakers were quick to give Cruickshank 120-to-1 odds, and likely laughed all the way to bank. But it was Cruickshank who got the last laugh when Jones accomplished the feat later that fall. The tidy payoff of $60,000 loomed even larger in the midst of the Great Depression.

With two championship courses the equal of any in Atlanta, an established winter resort business that attracted the nation's elite, and a moderate winter climate, Augusta was the logical choice as a location to build Jones' dream. Augusta, too, where Jones likely met and developed a longstanding friendship with Clifford Roberts, who was picked by Jones to handle the financial affairs of the new club. When Jones announced intentions in 1930 to build the dream course "near Augusta provided a suitable piece of ground might be available in that neighborhood," his words were met with obvious disappointment among Atlantans who had supported him throughout his career.

In early 1931 Thomas Barrett Jr., vice president of the Bon Air Vanderbilt and a Chamber of Commerce member, was consulted about available land in Augusta and he brought to attention the old Fruitlands Nurseries property. Curious about the lay of the land adjacent to the Augusta Country Club Jones decided to take a closer look.

Like the fortuitous meeting between Jones and MacKenzie in California in the fall of 1929, there was good fortune in securing the property that became the Augusta National Golf Club. It was fate that the 365 acres were even for sale at the time Bobby Jones was looking for a spot to put his golf course. Just five years earlier the same property was the projected site of a high-rise hotel and golf course by Commodore Perry

Founders Keepers, circa 1920s Bobby Jones and Clifford Roberts share a moment at the Bon Air Vanderbilt Hotel just blocks from where the course could be built. (© Historic Golf Photos–Ron Watts Collection.)

The Master Plan Bobby Jones (third from left, front row) and course designer Alister MacKenzie (third from left, back row) at a golf outing to form the Augusta National Golf Club. The group seated L-R includes Rex Cole (Rex Cole Refrigerator Corporation), M.H. Aylesworth (president of NBC), Jones, Kent Cooper (Associated Press), W. Alton "Pete" Jones (Cities Service Company); and standing L-R are Richard C. Patterson, Jr. (NYC Corrections Commissioner), John W. Harris (Hegeman-Harris Company), MacKenzie, Grantland Rice (Sportswriter), Alfred Severin Bourne (Singer Sewing Machine heir), Fielding Wallace (President of the Augusta Country Club and Secretary of the Augusta National Golf Club),and Clifford Roberts (Chairman of the Augusta National Golf Club).

Forest Foursome circa 1930 Bobby Jones is flanked by 1928 U. S. Open Champion Johnny Farrell, sportswriter Grantland Rice and baseball legend Ty Cobb at Forest Hills Golf Course, the site of his 13 shot margin of victory in the 1930 Southeastern Open. (Courtesy Forest Hills Golf Course.)

J. Stoltz. But in the wake of the Great Miami Hurricane of 1926, Stolz was forced to file for bankruptcy and the property reverted into the hands of the Washington Heights Development Company.

When Jones and partner Clifford Roberts stepped onto the grounds for the first time in the spring of 1931, they traversed the magnolia-lined entrance and viewed the vista that lay before them. It was then that

Jones remarked, "Perfect! And to think this ground has been lying around all these years waiting for someone to come along and lay a golf course on it." Jones encountered tough times in the form of the Great Depression that nearly ended his dream. In his book *The Story of the Augusta National*, Roberts recorded that had they known the Depression would drag on, "I am very certain that we would have called off the

Augusta National Golf Club Links
from Club House Veranda
Augusta, Georgia

Clubhouse Veranda Clubhouse view overlooking the ninth and eighteenth greens featured in the 1934 Augusta National Invitation Tournament program. (Photo by Tony Sheehan. Courtesy of Joseph M. Lee III.)

Despite the uncertainty of the times, an option on the land was taken for $70,000 on June 30, 1931, by a newly formed real estate company, the Fruitlands Manor Corporation.

project." But Jones' vision included a relatively unknown design architect named Alister MacKenzie with a track record for cost efficiency in addition to his artistry.

While Donald Ross' design work at two nearby Augusta courses and hundreds of others worldwide remains a testament to his skill and ingenuity, Bobby Jones was in search of something elusive, much like the Grand Slam he attained the previous year. And despite Ross' best intentions to persuade him otherwise, Jones went with a gut feeling like the one he had while touring Cypress Point and Pasatiempo two years before. This dream course in Augusta required Bobby Jones' own signature and he turned instead to the artistry of MacKenzie to build upon that vision. It was MacKenzie's grasp of subtle nuances in impacting the larger picture, cost efficiency, and immense reverence and knowledge of St. Andrews that likely turned the tide in his favor. Had the roles been reversed and MacKenzie been the one who had designed two previous courses in Augusta, only then might Ross have stood a better chance of Bobby Jones' blessing.

Despite the uncertainty of the times, an option on the land was taken for $70,000 on June 30, 1931, by a newly formed real estate company, the Fruitlands Manor Corporation. The group was comprised of Jones and his father, Colonel Robert P. Jones, Roberts,

Thomas Barrett Jr., Vanderbilt Hotel magnate Walton H. Marshall, and Augusta Country Club president Fielding Wallace.

The Fruitlands Manor Corporation leased the property to the Augusta National Golf Club, which was incorporated at the same time. An organizing committee of five was formed for the new club and charged with fundraising for the purpose of constructing Jones' golf course and with attracting prospective club members. The group included Jones, Roberts, sportswriter Grantland Rice, business executive William C. Watt, and heir to the Singer Sewing Machine fortune Alfred S. Bourne.

Though Bourne lost a fortune during the stock market crash and was sorry he could not fund the entire project, his pledge of $25,000 to be paid within a year went a long way toward the new club becoming reality. Vanderbilt Hotel chain owner Walton Marshall matched Bourne's pledge, and Watt and Wallace chipped in $5,000 each. The enterprise was off the ground but the new club had barely enough money to construct Jones' golf course. Securing enough members at $350 each to keep the dream alive proved a formidable task. But Jones had made his name in golf by staring down adversity and the Great Depression was just one more hurdle to be cleared.

Framing the Scene

When Alister MacKenzie came to Augusta to design Bobby Jones' dream golf course in 1931, Augusta had long been recognized as the nation's top winter resort and playground for the rich and famous. The setting was not uncommon to MacKenzie, whose design at Pasatiempo was a haven for stars in Hollywood and served as a working model for the Augusta National Golf Club.

A hot summer's day in mid-July is hardly the ideal time to plan a long walk through a forest of deep brush. But that is exactly what transpired on the morning of Tuesday, July 14, 1931, in Augusta as Alister MacKenzie and Bobby Jones made their historic first walk on the property of the old Fruitland Nurseries.

The survey group that accompanied MacKenzie and Jones consisted of Colonel Robert P. Jones, Prosper Julius Alphonse Berckmans and Louis Alphonse Berckmans (two of the three sons of the late Prosper Julius Berckmans and grandsons of the late Louis Mathieu Edouard Berckmans, who cofounded Fruitlands Nurseries in 1857), W. B. Marquis (from the Boston landscape engineering firm Olmstead Brothers), Wendell P. Miller (construction engineer), and Augustan Tony Sheehan. (Sheehan took what are believed to be the first photographs of the grounds, a number of which appeared in the Augusta National Invitation Tournament Program in 1934 and also appear in this book.) Over the course of three days, MacKenzie and Jones staked out the dream golf course at the Augusta National Golf Club.

As MacKenzie and Jones toured the grounds of the Augusta National for the first time, *Augusta Chronicle* sportswriter Harold Stephens was the proverbial fly on the wall for this telling page in golf history. Much can be gained from Stephens' observations as the two men walked the course together for the first time. In the following day's newspaper he noted that Jones and MacKenzie deemed the lay of the land ideal for a golf course and related that Jones proclaimed "When I come here, I'm going to play some golf!" According to Stephens, the pair agreed that the land was "great. There's nothing sensational about [the property], nothing that would make the course unusually difficult for the average player, but more than enough to give him satisfaction in his game—and to make an expert exert himself to bring in a winning score."

"Whoever cleared this land," Stephens quoted Jones, "must have had the idea of golf in mind. The woods are almost perfect for the game. Dr. MacKenzie's idea is that the course should be as natural as possible. We want to get as far away from anything artificial as we can. And from the looks of things we're going to be able to carry our ideas out."

Stephens continued, "Dr. MacKenzie and Jones found cause for elation in the layout of the land. They were armed with maps and blueprints, showing contours in detail, and a composite aerial photograph of the entire area. Penciled on them were tentative locations of fairways and greens, which they checked against conditions as they found them. Apparently few changes will be necessary in the completed plans."

Jones could already envision the championship golf to be played over the property and according to Stephens, "Bobby's eye's gleamed as he walked along, his imagination building the picture of the completed course." Stephens also reported overhearing Jones'

MacKenzie Drawing circa 1932

Dated 1932, this MacKenzie drawing shows the course routed in reverse order from his 1931 layout. The 1934 Augusta National Invitation Tournament was played with this routing. Bobby Jones reversed the design for good later that year.

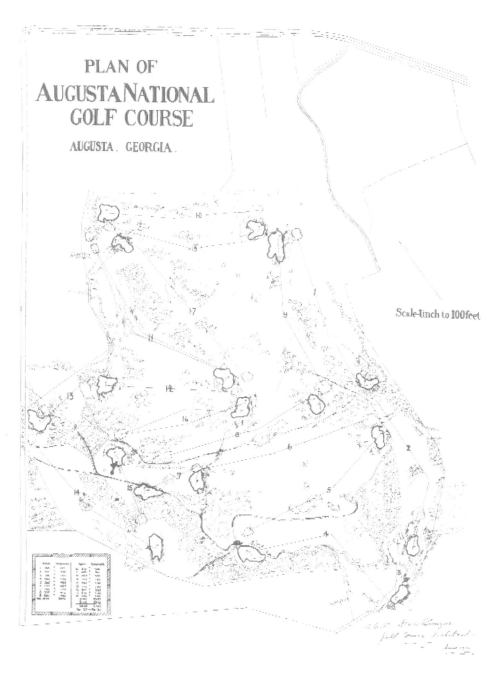

PLAN OF
AUGUSTA NATIONAL
GOLF COURSE

AUGUSTA, GEORGIA.

Scale 1inch to 100feet

According to Stephens, MacKenzie and company walked the grounds at a fast pace under a blazing July sun.

comment to MacKenzie, "Here's a peach of a hole, doctor—put the tee there; you go along the woods to a green over there under that group of pines. A good two-shotter, about two hundred and ninety yards. And from there down in to the hollow, with the green alongside that creek. It couldn't have been better fixed for it."

MacKenzie was also impressed with the landscape of the old Fruitlands Nurseries and Stephens noted: "His expert eye fastened onto every detail. Not a tree or a ridge or an undulation of the land escaped him." The perceptive Stephens went on to write that "He [MacKenzie]likes undulations—a fairway that drops a bit before the tee and then rises to give the ball a crest from which it can catch a roll. He called Bobby into frequent consultation; those trees there—do you think we ought to go over them or come in to the side?Between them, with the lay of the land spread out like a map, they would thresh it out."

According to Stephens, MacKenzie and company walked the grounds at a fast pace under a blazing July sun. Augustan Tony Sheehan could not take the intense heat and needed assistance to be taken off the grounds. Someone in the party remarked to Jones, "I don't see how you stand it bareheaded." Jones grinned and replied with a telling comment, "My skull's thick."

The headlines of the *Augusta Chronicle* of July 14, 1931, trumpeted: "BOBBY JONES TO BUILD HIS IDEAL GOLF COURSE ON BERCKMANS' PLACE." Atlanta sportswriter O. B. Keeler filed a report that day and quoted Jones as saying, "I am joining with a group of friends as one of the organizers of a new club to be known as the Augusta National Golf Club. It is strictly a private undertaking and is in no sense a commercial project. Although my time now is largely devoted to the business of law, and I have retired forever from competitive golf, this great game will always be my hobby, and my ambition in connection with the Augusta enterprise is to help build a course which may possibly be recognized as one of the great golf courses of the world.

"Augusta is in my home state. It has a singularly fine climate, and my experience in this city, in the Southeastern Open Championship last spring, convinced me that nowhere in this hemisphere was there anything to surpass the golfing conditions, turf, greens or climate, offered by this immediate locality.

"Of course I cannot deny that it is an idea very dear to my heart, to see in reality a golf course embodying the finest holes of all the great courses on which I have played. But I am not having this dream alone, or without the most expert collaboration. Dr. MacKenzie is the man who will actually design the course. His name needs no presentation to the American golfing public or the golfers of the world. I am happy to accompany him this morning on a tour of the property and to assume the role of consultant with him on this golf course. I know it is his ambition, and my earnest hope, to present a course that will find a place in North American golfing history as one of the layouts truly national in character and characteristics. English sportsmen and Canadians have been invited to join this club; and I am sure we shall have in Augusta a representative group of members from all over the world. This club, as I hope, is to be a truly national sports club."

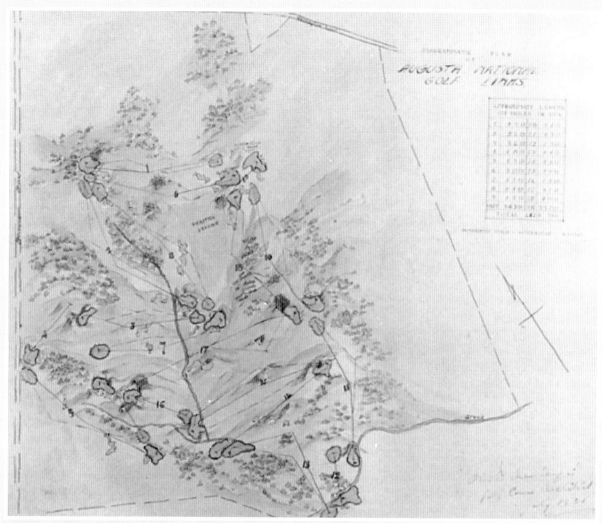

Original Layout circa 1931 This drawing by MacKenzie dated 1931 shows that the original layout of the Augusta National Golf Club was routed as it is today. MacKenzie personally gave the drawing to Jones and Jones donated it to his new law firm. The field of the 1934 Augusta National Invitation Tournament played the course in reverse order. (Courtesy of Alston & Bird LLP.)

MacKenzie and Jones no doubt discussed the idea and simply decided it made sense to reverse the nines.

If Jones could likely have done anything differently regarding the announcement it would have been to change the phrase "a golf course embodying the finest holes of all the great courses on which I have played." What he likely meant to announce was something more along the lines of "a golf course embodying the spirit of the finest holes." Jones spent much time over the years explaining away the notion that the layout was meant to copy other holes, which he and MacKenzie assuredly would never do. In MacKenzie's words, "I always attempt not only to make every hole different on a golf course, but never conspicuously reproduce two exactly similar holes."

The result of their three-day work in July 1931 yielded a 200:1 scale routing map signed by MacKenzie in which the holes were numbered in the order they are currently played. Within one year's time the plan for the course that bore MacKenzie's signature showed the holes numbered in reverse order, with the tenth hole to be the first. While much has been made of the change, this likely posed no controversy at all. As the Augusta National was finally cleared and fairways shaped, MacKenzie and Jones had a better view of the property and their perspective likely changed. Upon further review the duo apparently felt the current front side would provide for a more exciting closing nine. The up and down current ninth hole would certainly provide dramatic flair as the eighteenth hole.

MacKenzie and Jones no doubt discussed the idea and simply decided it made sense to reverse the nines.

They obviously did not take into account the ramifications of April frost along the steeper, shadier hole that became the first. They had no reason to. At the time, the Masters Tournament was not a consideration. The course remained in that configuration for the next two years, including for the first Augusta National Invitation Tournament, then was changed permanently back to the way MacKenzie and Jones had originally planned the layout. They also decided later to scale back (from thirty-six to twenty-two) the already sparse number of bunkers in the original plan. Bunkers were costly and they did not fit well with the plan for a pleasurable course for the largest number of golfers.

Based on Jones' good name alone, the buildup and instant notoriety for the proposed course was impressive. The Sunday, July 16, 1931, edition of the *Augusta Chronicle* noted that MacKenzie's and Jones' project "will be the world's premier golf links." The article went on to include, "It is expected that work will proceed throughout the fall and winter on this course for it to be ready by the winter of next year. The cost of the work do be done in the next eight to ten months will probably amount to a quarter of a million dollars."
The cost-effective measures employed by MacKenzie, coupled with low labor costs during the Great Depression, helped cut that estimate in half.

"With all of the financing out of the way, with ample funds provided to do that which he plans," the *Augusta Chronicle* of October 29, 1931, reported, "Bobby and Dr. Alister MacKenzie, the noted Scottish golf architect who has built more than 400 courses in Europe and America, have worked out plans with great care and now that they are complete, the work of the Miller Engineering Company, actual builders of the course, is ready to start."It was obvious the world had nary a clue that the Great Depression was also having a great negative impact financially on the new club on Washington Road. According to the newspaper, construction engineer Wendell Miller was scheduled to be in Augusta the following day and the Olmstead Brothers landscaping company was ready to begin work.

Miller and Olmstead were the same companies that constructed MacKenzie's layout at Pasatiempo that Jones liked so much. The Olmstead Brothers firm was owned by the sons of famous landscape architect Frederick Law Olmstead. Among other notable projects, the elder Olmstead designed the landscapes for Central Park, Vanderbilt's Biltmore Estate, the village of Pinehurst in North Carolina, the U.S. Capitol, and Stanford University. In Augusta, he also landscaped the lake area situated at the point where Washington Road today merges with the Calhoun Expressway just below the Augusta National. Named in his honor, Lake Olmstead takes in the water that flows from Rae's Creek.

Louis Alphonse Berckmans and younger brother Prosper Jr., whose family founded Fruitlands Nurseries nearly three-quarters of a century earlier, played major roles with the new club. Prosper Jr. supervised a crew that transplanted more than four thousand trees and shrubs on the new golf course. He later helped name each hole with a prevalent planting and served as the Augusta National's first general manager. Louis Alphonse became a member of the club's beautification committee.

By the time MacKenzie arrived in Augusta for a second visit in September 1931, pathways to the holes had been cleared. "Up until this time," the *Augusta Chronicle* reported in its update on the course, "the work of making contour maps and clearing away the vines and other undergrowth in the large forest on the Berckmans' tract have been the chief activities, but from now on the work should speed up and, as stated, the peak should be reached during March and April when there will be many winter visitors in the city." That is precisely the scenario that unfolded, but not before words were exchanged between club cofounder Clifford Roberts and architect Alister MacKenzie.

After MacKenzie returned to California to work on other projects in the fall of 1931, Roberts reportedly called into question MacKenzie's best effort at creating Jones' dream. When Roberts wrote MacKenzie in December that a final meeting to determine the status of the Augusta National was scheduled for early January 1932, MacKenzie hinted that associate Marion Hollins would make the trip in his stead. The 1921 U.S. Women's Amateur champion, Hollins had worked alongside MacKenzie at Cypress Point and hired him to design her golf course at Pasatiempo and he was confident in her design abilities. MacKenzie also remained occupied by other work and had yet to be paid any advance monies for work in Augusta. He also sensed that in the wake of hard financial times the club was still not fully committed to the project. MacKenzie viewed the Depression not as a setback but an opportunity to construct the Augusta National at an even lower cost and he informed Roberts of such. MacKenzie even cut his $10,000 design fee in half in hopes it would help keep the project alive.

It was Hollins who eventually made the trip to Augusta in January 1932 and reported favorably on the work being done there. When MacKenzie returned to Augusta for a third time in the spring of 1932, he oversaw the final delicate work to putting surfaces.

Father and Son circa 1933
Standing outside the clubhouse, Bobby Jones looks the course over with his father Colonel Robert P. Jones. (Courtesy of Western Golf Association.)

Under Construction, circa 1932 Sand from the Atlantic coast was transported to Augusta for use in bunkers and on greens. The sand was mixed with sedge peat (middle of photo) to comprise topsoil that was plowed into putting surfaces. (Courtesy of Western Golf Association.)

The Masterpiece Takes Shape

According to MacKenzie, "To obtain the best possible results at a minimum of cost is the guiding principle of golf course construction." Ever the design strategist and tactician, MacKenzie staunchly maintained that "the value of a golf course is measured by the mental labor put into it, and not by the manual labor and materials." He felt he could accomplish twice as much at half the cost, utilize less labor and more mental effort in the process, eschew the artificial, and let nature create the gem.

MacKenzie prided himself on the fact that he never accepted a design project that took more than $100,000 to complete. With that figure in mind, he began work on the Augusta National. He came close to delivering the course at that amount, despite an additional $15,000 in upgrades. A proponent of the less-is-more theory of course design, the cost-efficient MacKenzie was true to his word that, "Five thousand dollars in labor expended under expert supervision is better than a hundred thousand injudiciously expended." Only when one considers that the actual playing surface of the new course was fully twice that of the average course of its day can MacKenzie's work be fully appreciated.

In 1932 the Augusta National's robust eighty acres of fairway space was more than double the size of most courses. The same went for its putting surfaces that equaled more than 100,000 square feet, a number that did not include 16,000 square feet in collars around the eighteen greens. In essence, MacKenzie and Jones created one grand golf course over the space that was typically reserved for two 18-hole layouts.

Despite the tough financial times, the Augusta

Clearing the Way During the fall of 1931 trees were cleared from the grounds of the old Fruitlands Nurseries to make way for Bobby Jones' dream golf course. (© of Historic Golf Photos–Ron Watts Collection.)

National paid its laborers twice the going rate during the Great Depression. In his book *Golf Architecture*, MacKenzie stressed, "In actual practice, experience has taught us that a few extra cents paid in men's wages is worth many dollars in actual production." Construction engineer Wendell Miller was instructed to pay nonskilled laborers one dollar per day for working "can to can't," or from the time they could see sunlight

Keeping up with the Joneses circa 1932 Bobby Jones hits golf balls at the 8th hole while the course was under construction. Colonel Robert P. Jones, Clifford Roberts, and course designer Alister McKenzie take note. (© Historic Golf Prints - Ron Watts Collection)

until they could not see at all. According to cofounder Clifford Roberts in his book *The Story of the Augusta National Golf Club*, on one occasion a contract was let out to the lowest bidder and laborers were unknowingly paid fifty cents a day. But according to Roberts, even that amount was double what many workers on area farms were being paid during the hard times.

Utilizing this cost-efficient labor force and aided with machinery in the form of tractors, earthmovers, and scrapers pulled by mule, MacKenzie went to work on his masterpiece. In less than three months' time

work crews under the direction of Miller moved 120,000 cubic yards of soil, and MacKenzie defined the course layout. According to two-time Masters champion (1984 and 1995) Ben Crenshaw, "MacKenzie and Jones selected Miller because he could make the ground function the way they wanted." In just 76 working days, 124 days total from the first shovel of dirt taken February 10, 1932, until the course was spread with 8,000 pounds of Scott's bermudagrass seed on May 27, 1932, MacKenzie delivered Bobby Jones' dream golf course.

When it debuted in 1932, the Augusta National was one of only several courses in the world with a state-of-the-art underground sprinkler system.

While the camouflage artist in MacKenzie honed in on his quality-over-quantity system of course design, Jones concentrated on the many potential club members with limited golf talent: "We want to make bogeys easy if frankly sought, pars readily obtainable by standard good play, and birdies, except on par fives, dearly bought." Hazards on MacKenzie layouts were used sparingly and not to penalize golfers, but merely to interject strategy. At the same time, MacKenzie wanted the course to give the illusion of being harder to play for the majority of golfers than it actually was.

What could be more challenging for the duo than to create a championship course for professionals coupled with a fun design for amateurs of all skill levels? Tee to green, the better the golfer the harder the course played. As MacKenzie sculpted a layout that would play to what he termed "equal 4s" (par 72) overall, he left it to Jones to affix the appropriate par status of each hole.

The result was a course with wide open fairways, large inviting greens, a minimum of bunkers, and no rough. The great equalizers were undulating fairways and slick putting surfaces that would strike a rare balance in challenging and accommodating golfers of all skill levels. For the first time, strategically placed bunkers came more into play for the long-ball hitter than those with mid-to-average length off the tee. MacKenzie's strategic design challenged the more skillful golfer and engaged the thinking man.

MacKenzie's last trip to Augusta was in the spring of 1932, just prior to the seeding of the Augusta National. It was then that the exacting undulations to the putting sur-faces were put in place. "They dipped the ground out and excavated 80 to 100 yards in front of the green," two-time Masters champion and golf historian Ben Crenshaw noted. "They were trying to move water and to just barely undulate the ground, to make the ground more alive. At the same time, this gave them the earth they needed to shape the green."

It was also during his final trip to Augusta that MacKenzie was approached about the revision and installation of grass greens at the nearby Palmetto Golf Club. A handful of members from the Aiken, South Carolina, course were also charter members of Jones' new club in Augusta. They made quick note that the historic first golf course in the southeast was the only area course still outfitted with sand putting surfaces. Palmetto raised $25,000 for the project and MacKenzie and contractor Wendell Miller reportedly volunteered their efforts.

When it debuted in 1932, the Augusta National was one of only several courses in the world with a state-of-the-art underground sprinkler system. Thirty-two thousand feet of cast-iron pipe ran the length of its fairways and greens, and a line feeding unfiltered water between the Savannah River and Augusta reservoir was tapped near the fifth hole to provide flow. The original system

remained in place for forty years before it was in need of being replaced with modern polyvinyl chloride (PVC) pipe in the early 1970s.

With its Buckner hoseless watering system spouting river water through sprinkler heads in 200-foot circles, the 8,000 pounds of Scott's bermudagrass seeded on fairways took root quickly. The Augusta National was mowed for the first time on June 10. By late August Bobby Jones teed it up for the first time and reportedly posted an even par 72. Local members played the course at year's end and the formal opening was scheduled for January 13, 1933. The Augusta National was over-seeded with Italian rye and a lush green paradise greeted guests for the occasion.

Not only did MacKenzie make good on his design of an eighteen-hole golf course for Jones, but also included at Jones' request a short nineteenth hole in the original design. The hole provided a last chance for golfers to even their wagers on the day and came in especially handy during the club's grand opening celebration. The nineteenth hole was situated to the back of the ninth and eighteenth greens, where the practice putting surface is currently located. On the day the course officially opened in January 1933, the *Augusta Chronicle* made note: "Outstanding is the nineteenth hole—actually where ties are played off." The following year the hole's putting surface began use as the practice putting green for the Invitation Tournament.

Early plans reportedly also called for a second smaller eighteen-hole "ladies" course to be built, but the idea, like a 500-yard, 9-hole chip-and-putt course later proposed by MacKenzie, was vetoed. In 1933 MacKenzie designed an eighteen-hole par-3 course that measured 2,460 yards, but again Jones reneged. Limited funds and Jones' focus on the main course, which was double the size of courses of the day, were likely determining factors.

Finally in 1958, during better times, architect George Cobb designed the nine-hole course with input from Clifford Roberts. Two new holes were added by Tom Fazio in 1986 to play over Ike's Pond. The original starting holes are still maintained but are no longer utilized during the annual Par-3 Contest on Wednesdays during Masters Week. Like the main course, the Augusta National Golf Club's eleven-hole par-3 layout has also been outfitted with an underground sprinkler system.

An area of interest that the founding fathers of the Augusta National briefly entertained was the growing trend of property development on golf courses. During his initial tour of the land with MacKenzie in 1931, Jones indicated an early interest in building a home on the property. But the only buyer to ever come forward was Augustan W. Montgomery Harison who purchased three lots to the back and side of the first green. Harison had his residence constructed there and one of his sons built a smaller home nearby.

Though he pulled off the most famous shot in Masters history, Gene Sarazen did not share MacKenzie's and Jones' zeal for the original layout. In Curt Sampson's *The Masters, Golf, Money and Power in Augusta*, Georgia, Sarazen is quoted as saying much later about the course, "No, I wasn't impressed. I didn't care for it. It was not a good course when Jones and MacKenzie finished it—a very poor design. Hell, number eleven was a drive and a pitch. They used to drive theseventh hole. Sixteen was a terrible hole, one

Palmetto Course Aerial view of Palmetto Golf Club where Alister MacKenzie redesigned the layout following his work at the Augusta National Golf Club. (Courtesy of Palmetto Golf Club.)

hundred yards over a ditch. And the first hole should have been like St. Andrews' (wide open) first, but it wasn't anything like it."Others reportedly took exception that the course favored Jones' high hook and perhaps exposed weaknesses in their own games. Welcome to Bobby Jones' golf course.

Constructive criticism of early design features aside, from a scoring standpoint, besting "Old Man Par" at the Augusta National in the 1930s was cause for celebration. While an unprecedented ten golfers, Sarazen included, broke par during the first round of the 1935 Augusta National Invitation Tournament, only five managed to finish under par for the week. In fact, during the first five Invitation Tournaments combined

As the Great Depression dragged on, it was also responsible for the greatly reduced number of entries in the tournament, which paid money only to the top twelve finishers.

(1934 to 1938) just nineteen golfers finished under par through four rounds of regulation play. As a comparison, thirty players accomplished the feat in the 2001 event alone, the last tournament prior to major course changes.

MacKenzie did not survive to see the Augusta National play to tournament conditions. Without his input, Jones took advice from peers, some of whom knew little of, and likely cared less for, MacKenzie's philosophies. It was also during this time at the height of the Great Depression that the Augusta National could least afford to make major changes to the course. It should also be noted that Sarazen's early thoughts about the course were among the first to be accepted.

As the Great Depression dragged on, it was also responsible for the greatly reduced number of entries in the tournament, which paid money only to the top twelve finishers. In the span of just five years, the field had dwindled from seventy-two golfers for the opening event in 1934 to just forty-six participants in 1939. Finally, in 1940, the club began showing signs of recovery, but by then the winds of war were close at hand. The Augusta National Golf Club canceled its tournament for three years during World War II and was forced to restart its climb to prominence after the war.

With the exception of Bobby Jones, the early years of the fledgling Augusta National were every bit an optical illusion as MacKenzie's golf course. Clifford Roberts proved a master at juggling payroll, finance efforts, and construction deals that helped keep the project afloat. Roberts' sleight of hand helped stretch the limited dollars even farther.

"One thing in our favor," Roberts noted in his book, *The Story of the Augusta National Golf Club*, "was the opportunity to make each dollar do double duty as the result of so many business people wanting to be identified with Bobby's course." An abundance of raw materials that included loads of humus from Florida, an intricate underground watering system, sand from the Atlantic seaboard, and plentiful amounts of grass seed were either donated or purchased below cost. What was not utilized in Augusta was sent along to the next job site at Palmetto Golf Club.

Following completion of work in Augusta, equipment and excess supplies were sent immediately to nearby Aiken, South Carolina, for MacKenzie's redesign and conversion to grass greens. While construction of the Augusta National proved a model of cost efficiency, Palmetto established a record for redesign cost that will likely never be challenged. Able to take advantage of its proximity to Augusta, Palmetto purchased excess goods from the new club at reduced costs. MacKenzie's redesign plans for Palmetto called for grass putting surfaces to be established and the course lengthened

"It must demand study, strategy as well as skill, otherwise it cannot be enduringly interesting."

from 5,833 to 6,370 yards. The work was completed at Palmetto in 1933, the year after the Augusta National was finished. In the final equation, MacKenzie designed two historic courses in the Augusta area that equaled the size of three. The construction cost of the two projects combined was slightly more than $125,000, frugal even by 1930s standards.

In mid-August 1932 the *New York Times* ran a feature story on the new course. The hometown newspaper for a majority of prospective charter members of the Augusta National, the *Times* featured an article entitled, "A Golf Course for the Forgotten Man." Pictures of Jones and the construction site were featured along with details of his design philosophies. "There are at least four essentials that go into the making of an ideal golf course," Jones remarked. "To be really great a golf course must be pleasurable to the greatest possible number of players, regardless of their ability. It must demand study, strategy as well as skill, otherwise it cannot be enduringly interesting. It must give the average player a fair chance and at the same time require the utmost from the expert who tries for sub-par scores. All natural beauty must be preserved, natural hazards should be utilized and artificiality reduced to a minimum." His dream course sculpted by MacKenzie at the Augusta National qualified on all four counts.

"For the average player," Jones continued, "there is nothing more disheartening than the appearance of a carry which is beyond his best effort and no alternative route offered. Dr. MacKenzie and I have tried hard to avoid that on the National, and I think we have been successful."

For MacKenzie there was likely nothing more disheartening than having to prod Roberts for a paycheck. On one occasion when Roberts questioned the architect's expenses, MacKenzie wrote him back in jest, "What an infernal trouble you are! I suppose the mere fact that you are making yourself a damned nuisance to me is an indication of your value to the Augusta National."

By late 1932, long after the course was complete, MacKenzie had received only $2,000 of his already greatly reduced fees. At wits end, MacKenzie wrote Roberts stating, "I am at the end of my tether; no one has paid me a cent since last June. We have mortgaged everything we have and have not yet been able to pay the nursing expenses of my wife's operation. Can you possibly let me have, at any rate $500 to keep me out of the poor house?" Back at the Augusta National Golf Club things were no longer running on a shoestring but hanging by a thread. In early 1933 foreclosure on the property weighed heavily on Roberts' mind.

Reportedly fearing foreclosure on his own home, MacKenzie wrote Roberts again seeking money, though his plea was not without his usual humor: "For some time I have been reduced to playing golf with four clubs and a Woolworth ball." He finally convinced Roberts to issue short-term notes that helped secure

Palmetto Marker Palmetto Golf Club in Aiken, South Carolina, is the oldest golf course in the southeastern United States and was redesigned by Alister MacKenzie when his work at Augusta National was complete. (Courtesy of Palmetto Golf Club.)

MacKenzie's home on the golf course at Pasatiempo. Roberts did so on the condition that MacKenzie not redeem the club's notes in Augusta where they would be recognized as having little or no value.

Later that year, MacKenzie's life took a sudden turn for the worse. On the last day of 1933 he suffered a coronary thrombosis at home and never recovered. He did not live to see the Augusta National in its finished state, let alone receive full payment for his work. Still, MacKenzie must have known upon completion that he and Jones had designed a course that would stand for the ages. In doing so he not only fulfilled Jones' dream but his own hence he referred to the Augusta National as "my best opportunity, and I believe, my finest achievement."

When working in Augusta, MacKenzie and wife Hilda took up residence at the Bon Air Vanderbilt in the "Hill Section," just blocks from the Augusta National. Like other grand hotels in the resort city, the Bon Air featured popular dance bands for its guests. The MacKenzie's are reported to have ruled the dance floor. "Ladies and gentlemen, we focus your attention on the center of the ballroom for the MacKenzies of Santa Cruz, California." Picture if you will Alister and Hilda strategically high stepping to music in front of a packed audience. At precisely the right moment the MacKenzie's would likely interject a spectacular dance step woven succinctly into their routine of understated elegance, a step designed to bring down the house. It was classic MacKenzie.

Artwork on Display

Alister MacKenzie finished Bobby Jones' dream in record time, and the course was playable by August 1932. By year's end the Augusta National Golf Club was frequented by local members and it was decided that a formal opening should occur very early in 1933. Friday the 13th in January was selected as the date of the celebration. It should be of no surprise that an unlucky and untimely spell of bad weather accompanied the event.

According to Clifford Roberts in his book *The Story of the Augusta National*, he and sportswriter Grantland Rice put together a package to bring charter members and guests to inaugurate Jones' dream golf course in style. Jones and local members Thomas Barrett Jr. and Fielding Wallace also juggled a major load of the grand opening responsibilities.

Ten thousand dollars went a long way during the Depression. One hundred dollars is what each of the one hundred charter members and guests paid for the three-day junket to Augusta from the northeast. The dollar figure included railway transportation and three days' lodging at the Vanderbilt Bon Air. The grand opening celebration consisted mainly of three groups. Clifford Roberts hosted the "Northeast Group," Grantland Rice accompanied an early-to-arrive "Eastern Group," and Jones held sway with a third "Atlanta Group."

Roberts' party on wheels rolled out of Penn Station in New York City on Thursday, January 12, 1933, and made stops in Philadelphia and Baltimore en route to Augusta. The train load of charter members and guests of the Augusta National traveled in style. As related in *The Story of the Augusta National*, the group was treated to a pair of new dining cars, club cars, and new Pullman equipment for the journey.

When the northeast group arrived in Augusta's Union Station at 9 A.M. the following morning, the weather was unseasonably cold. As they stepped into the near-freezing temperatures, many likely did a double take to make sure they were actually in Augusta, Georgia, and not Augusta, Maine. In an effort to take full advantage of grand opening festivities, the group had donned golf attire while on the train. As the assembly was shuttled to the Augusta National Golf Club, their luggage was routed to quarters at the luxurious Bon Air Vanderbilt on "The Hill."

By the time Roberts' northeast group arrived at the golf course that morning, the two other smaller parties were already on the course. Grantland Rice's eastern group had arrived by train two days earlier and Jones' Atlanta group on Thursday. Major champion Francis Ouimet (U.S. Open, 1913; U.S. Amateur, 1914 and 1931) checked in for the gala event on Thursday evening. Another international golf star of the day, Jess Sweetser, was also in attendance.

According to newspaper accounts, Jones and Rice greeted each foursome as they arrived at the tee on Friday. Jones did not play golf that morning as he had teed it up in the first foursome to go out the previous day. "In spite of the poor golfing weather," the *Augusta Chronicle* reported, "the atmosphere at the National was one of jovial comradeship with financiers, capitalists, businessmen, and brokers all talking golf." While Augusta was spared the ice and snow that hit other areas of the south, the rain and bitter cold could not have been much better. Roberts was asked his opinion

Welcome to Augusta! circa 1933
Augustan Fielding Wallace (center) welcomes refrigerator mogul Rex Cole and publishing magnate B.C. Forbes for grand opening festivities of the Augusta National Golf Club, January 13-15, 1933. (Courtesy Western Golf Association.)

Drawing the most praise in MacKenzie's design of the Augusta National was the lack of bunkers coupled with the creative use of mounding and undulations.

of the occasion and replied, "Do you mean the course or the weather? You can't print what I think about the weather, but the entire affair is splendid. All we can ask for."

The majority of the northeast group played an entire round of golf and then "helped themselves to the barbeque on the front lawn under a large tent before starting out for a second eighteen holes in the afternoon."In his book *The Story of the Augusta National*, Roberts noted that a keg of corn whiskey at the start of each nine helped keep the party in good spirits. A handful of members in this group called it quits after nine holes and opted instead for the warmth and comfort of the Vanderbilt Bon Air. Jones spent part of the afternoon in front of a fireplace in the club office where he discussed business with Roberts.

A small number of wives accompanied their husbands on the historic trip and were also content to socialize in the Augusta National Clubhouse. According to newspaper reports, one woman in the group proclaimed, "There are no ladies on this trip. You see, many of the men told their wives there would be no wives on the trip and left them at home as golf widows while they are down here. But some of the wives sneaked off and joined the party. But we are good sports and don't want the wives back North to know we are having the time of our lives in the South."

MacKenzie's design was likely paid some of the highest compliments he ever received during the event. A keen advertising executive from New York observed, "The skyline hazard is the most effective I have seen. That's a good work and it isn't copyrighted. It tells exactly the effect of the design on the game of golf over this course." "Most magnificent," another golfer replied. "It has restored my pleasure in golf."

Drawing the most praise in MacKenzie's design of the Augusta National was the lack of bunkers coupled with the creative use of mounding and undulations. A pair of USGA officials on hand for the grand opening raved about the new course in the *New York Times* of Tuesday, January 17, 1933. Vice president of the organization, John G. Jackson, remarked that "the course is almost certain to have a far-reaching effect on future designing of golf courses in this country. I think that something quite new has been produced by Bobby. There is everywhere in evidence the affection that he holds for the old course at St. Andrews. His use of mounds through the fairway and

In an all too brief moment, Jones turned back the hands of time and blistered the course with a round of 69.

around the greens brings about an effect similar to the dunes at St. Andrews and on other seaside courses in the old country."

"This use of mounds instead of traps as is the general practice here," Jackson continued, "carries out the same general effect and will result in quite a saving in upkeep. I see no reason why first-class golf courses cannot be built along these lines and maintained at much less cost." USGA treasurer Archie M. Reid echoed the sentiments when he referred to construction at the Augusta National as "a unique job" and "a great golf course." Reid was most impressed with the design feature of putting surfaces which were unique for an inland golf course of the day: "They are like St. Andrews, big rolling greens with interesting contours and almost no trapping. In order to be reasonably certain of getting down in two putts you've got to watch your step carefully. You've got to come into the hole the correct way or else you are going to find yourself taking an extra putt to get down."

With MacKenzie absent from opening ceremonies, even more credit seemed to go in Jones' direction for the course's design. Though it was never mentioned in newspaper reports, an educated guess is that MacKenzie declined to attend the grand opening because he likely could not afford the trip from the West Coast. He did intend on attending the first Augusta National Invitation Tournament the following year and report-

edly would have been happy to take up quarters in the clubhouse if the club would pay his train fare to Augusta. Unfortunately for MacKenzie, he never saw the course in playing condition.

The headline spread across the front page of the *Augusta Chronicle* on Saturday, January 14, 1932, offered little reassurance about the weather: "Snow and Ice Bombardment Routs South's Spring Weather". Neither did the accompanying front-page story: "Winter's Unexpected Thrust Disrupts Tournament Plans Opening Up National Golf." But the untimely weather was hardly a nuisance for the many visitors from the north who took the cold in stride. After another full day of golf on Saturday, a banquet under the direction of Roberts was staged at the Bon Air Vanderbilt. Grantland Rice's Eastern Group had already departed for a fishing and swimming trip to Miami prior to returning home.

On Sunday, January 15, the third and final day of the gala event, Bobby Jones finally got a chance to relax a bit from the pressures of playing host and settled into the more comfortable role of playing golf. In an all too brief moment, Jones turned back the hands of time and blistered the course with a round of 69. The man who transformed the game of golf had given the dream course at Augusta National his personal stamp of approval.

Friday the 13th circa 1933 The official grand opening of the Augusta National Golf Club was held in spite of frigid weather that gripped the south on the weekend of January 13-15, 1933. (Courtesy Western Golf Association.)

At Home circa 1932 MacKenzie lived the final years of his life in California with his wife Hilda, close to the courses he designed at Pasatiempo and Cypress Point. (Courtesy Western Golf Association.)

The Final Act

For Alister MacKenzie, the end came prematurely. At sixty-three years of age he had just begun to hit his stride as a celebrated golf architect. MacKenzie did not survive to see the completed version of the Augusta National or the redesign of nearby Palmetto Golf Club in Aiken and others. At his home on the sixth fairway at Pasatiempo, on New Year's Eve, 1933, MacKenzie suffered an attack from a blocked artery to his heart . One week later, while confined to bed, MacKenzie breathed his last with wife Hilda at his side.

MacKenzie was neither rich nor famous when he died and was owed thousands of dollars in golf course design fees. Shortly after his death MacKenzie's widow reportedly wrote Clifford Roberts with best wishes on the upcoming inaugural Invitation Tournament and ended her letter, "I know you will all wish Alister were there." Roberts wrote a return correspondence following the tournament which he detailed information of the events success and expressed optimism that he might soon be able to send money that was still owed MacKenzie.

A man with a penchant for perfection, Roberts had high marks for MacKenzie's work and likely summed up best the architect's vision when he wrote years later: "What a pity MacKenzie did not come to this country earlier or did not live for another ten years. We surely would have had many really interesting and pleasurable courses."

MacKenzie's name was only rarely mentioned in the Augusta newspapers while alive and even less in the years immediately following his death. While he sculpted the landscape that forever changed Augusta's destiny, MacKenzie's work was truly viewed as Jones' dream and golf course. Though Jones continually noted that he played only an associate's role to MacKenzie's brilliance, he has likely been given equal credit for the design.

Jones and Roberts have plaques at the end of Magnolia Lane, Jack Nicklaus and Arnold Palmer have tributes on the course. Sarazen, Ben Hogan, and Byron Nelson have bridges. President Dwight D. Eisenhower has a tree, pond, and cabin. MacKenzie is a trivia question. Only a fairway bunker at the tenth hole, large in stature but of little consequence, has any connection to the architect and the course he built in Augusta. "MacKenzie's mounds" surrounding the eighth green represent more a signature of his tactical, artistic, and cost-cutting genius at work. Still, due in part to brilliant manuscripts and revolutionary designs that have stood the test of time, MacKenzie is gone but hardly forgotten.

It was in 1994 that MacKenzie's lost manuscript was uncovered by his step-grandson, Raymund M. Haddock. At first glance Haddock thought the papers were MacKenzie's ancient articles regarding camouflage tactics. But closer inspection of the artifacts revealed a manuscript that lay camouflaged in his files for sixty years.

The recovery of the document proved fitting in that MacKenzie's manuscript remained dormant for so long and right in front of his family's eyes. Truth is, MacKenzie's genius was not fully appreciated until years after his death, and the rush to find the manuscript even by family members was not an urgent matter. Not until a renewed interest in his work nearly a half-century later was MacKenzie's manuscript even missed.

Like fine wine, MacKenzie's artistry finally came of age in the late-twentieth century. There were clues like one in his obituary that suggested another book had been written by the architect, but until Haddock's discovery, no evidence backed the claim. When efforts between 1978 and 1982 to locate the document came up empty, it was generally conceded that the work was lost for good.

But like the many golfers who have strained for clues to MacKenzie's golf riddle at the Augusta National, the obvious had been there all along. It is a role MacKenzie would likely have relished, being a major part of the puzzle within eyes view and still neatly tucked out of sight. MacKenzie made a living in that fashion and even in death the legacy continued.

The following obituary appeared in the *Santa Cruz Sentinel* shortly after MacKenzie's death in January 1934.

Dr. Alister MacKenzie, internationally famous golf architect, author and founder of the Camouflage School, England, which all officers of the allied forces during the World War attended to learn camouflage, died early yesterday afternoon at his home in Pasatiempo. He was 63 years of age, a native of Scotland, and had resided in this city since March, 1930.

Funeral services will be held Tuesday at 11 o'clock, with Rev. Norman H. Snow of the Episcopal church officiating. Internment will be in the Odd Fellows' mausoleum. Eventually the ashes will be sent to Dr. MacKenzie's old home in Scotland.

Dr. MacKenzie came back to the United States in 1927 especially to lay out the Cypress Point Golf Course. In 1929 he came to Santa Cruz and laid out the Pasatiempo Course. He married Mrs. Edgar Haddock during that year and in

1930 built the home in which he died. He had been ill only a short time and had been confined to his bed only two days. Surviving are the following: Mrs. MacKenzie, widow; two sisters, Miss Mabie MacKenzie and Dr. Marion MacKenzie; a stepson, G. Marston Haddock of San Francisco; Mrs. Haddock and two children.

Dr. MacKenzie had laid out and completed over 400 golf courses in England, Scotland, Australia, New Zealand and the United States, and was considered one of the best golf architects. He was consulting architect for the Royal and Ancient Golf Club of St. Andrews, Scotland. Among the principal in this country planned and laid out by him were Cypress Point, Pasatiempo and Augusta National. He also laid out the Buenos Aires Jockey Club at Buenos Aires.

Dr. MacKenzie had just finished a book on golf, entitled The Spirit of St. Andrews. *This book had not yet been published. He was working on a book of camouflage at the time of his death. The introduction of* The Spirit of St. Andrews *was written by Bobby Jones, internationally famed golfer.*

Despite information in his obituary to the contrary, according to certified birth records, MacKenzie was born in England. While he spoke with a deep Scottish brogue and considered himself as such down to the kilt he proudly wore, Scotland was the native land of MacKenzie's father.

While MacKenzie attested to more than 400 golf designs, and his obituary reiterated the same, only about 150 can actually be traced back to him. In true MacKenzie design mode, the quantity of his work may be limited, but the quality of his work stands as evidence to his greatness. While the Augusta National, Cypress Point, and Royal Melbourne are considered his greatest works, at least a dozen others, including his design at Pasatiempo, are worthy of "major" status, the golf term associated with greatness.

1907 Moortown Golf Club
Leeds, West Yorkshire, England
Host site of the 1929 Ryder Cup Matches.

1927 Blairgowrie Golf Club
(Rosemount Course)
Perthshire, Scotland
One of the top-rated golf courses in Scotland.

1927 Lahinch Golf Club, Old Course
County Clare, Ireland
Mackenzie redesign of Old Tom Morris'
original layout.

1928 The Valley Club of Montecito
Santa Barbara, California

1928 Cypress Point Club
Pebble Beach, California
Monterey Peninsula provides stunning
backdrop for this most scenic test in golf
history. Ranks as one of the top five courses
in the world.

1929 Pasatiempo Golf Club
Santa Cruz, California
Golf Digest (2004 Rankings) Top 100
American Golf Courses and Top 20 among
American Golf Courses open to the public.

1931 Royal Melbourne Golf Club
(West Course)
Black Rock, Victoria, Australia
Considered the best golf course south of
the equator.

1933 Augusta National Golf Club
Augusta, Georgia
Bobby Jones' dream course and site of the
Masters Tournament.

1933 Crystal Downs Country Club
Frankfort, Michigan
One of the top classical (pre-1960) designs in
the United States.

1939 Ohio State University Course
(Scarlet Course)
Columbus, Ohio
Golf Digest's pick as the top collegiate facility
in the United States. Host site of numerous
NCAA Championships and collegiate home of
six-time Masters champion Jack Nicklaus.

MacKenzie Bunker, circa 1994 The tenth hole
putting surface looking toward the fairway that
features the large MacKenzie Bunker. (Courtesy
of Michael O'Byrne Photography.)

Augusta National Golf Club, circa 1940
Early aerial photograph of Augusta National when Magnolia Lane was not yet paved and there were no cottages. (© Historic Golf Photos–Ron Watts Collection.)

The Front Nine

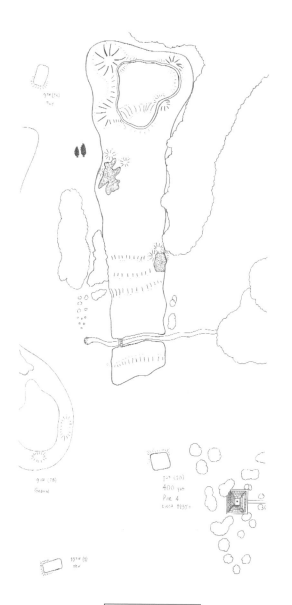

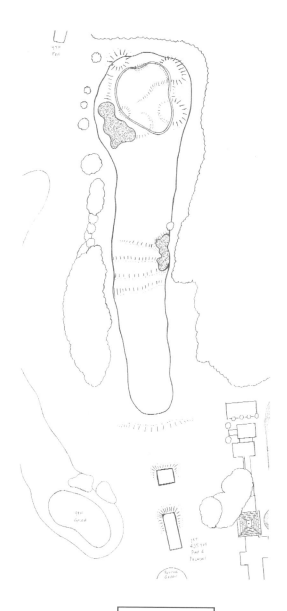

CIRCA 1930s

PRESENT

HOLE 1
Opening Act

Hole 1, circa 1934 For the first Augusta National Invitation Tournament in 1934, this hole marked the start of the back nine. Note the many fingers in the MacKenzie designed fairway bunker that was moved greenside in 1951. (Photo by Tony Sheehan. Courtesy of Joseph M. Lee III.)

MAJOR CHANGES

1951
Drainage pipe installed and ditch running along fairway at the bottom of the hill filled in.

1951
Left greenside bunker added.

1951
Section of landing area regraded.

1980
Tee box lengthened.

2002
Right-side fairway bunker redesigned to extend 10–15 yards closer to the green and tee box moved back 20–25 yards.

par	4	
1934 yardage	400	
1959 yardage	400	TEA OLIVE
current yardage	435	
difficulty	7	

Blessings from Above, circa 1940s Rare early view from the first fairway looking back toward the ninth green. Note the wooden footbridge that was put in place shortly after Alister MacKenzie designed the course. The ditch in the fairway was covered over in 1951. (Courtesy of Summerville Photo.)

"Ordinarily, the fairway bunker on the right presents no problem for the tournament player. With a heavy wind against, however, a half-hit tee shot may catch this bunker. At the same time, a drive down the right side of the fairway is only important when the wind is behind and the hole is cut immediately behind the bunker at the left front of the green. The player who drives down the left side must play his second either over the bunker or into the slopes which tend to direct the ball off the right side of the green."

—BOBBY JONES, 1959

Hole History

Originally known as Cherokee Rose, the hole was renamed Tea Olive for the prominent planting along the hole. For the first Augusta National Invitation Tournament in 1934, Bobby Jones reversed Alister MacKenzie's original design, marking this hole as the start of the back nine that year. MacKenzie's original design included a left-side fairway bunker that fell far short of the green. Also present in the tournament's early years was a trench that stretched across the fairway bottom approximately 75 yards from the tee. After hitting drives at the first tee, golfers crossed the trench over narrow wooden footbridges.

In 1951 the left-side fairway bunker was moved greenside and the ditch at the bottom of the tee was filled in as part of the construction plan for a Quonset hut for the media. A new tournament tee box was installed for the 2002 Masters that lengthened the hole by 25 yards and brought the right-side fairway bunker back into play.

Anything less than a 300-yard carry off the tee will not clear the hazard, forcing most golfers in the field to play it safe on this crucial first hole. A landing area to the left of the bunker is accommodating, but go too far left and a tree line beckons from the opposite side of the fairway. Recent changes call for longer, more strategic approach shots to an undulating putting surface guarded by a left greenside bunker. Threes are rare here and approaches that miss left or long can be extremely costly. One of the most difficult holes on the front side, the first hole played as the hardest hole on the entire course during the 2004 Masters.

Memorable Moments

Gary Player's steady play at the first hole in the 1961 Masters Tournament gave him early momentum and a distinct edge on the field. Playing the first hole in a record 3-under par for the week, Player won the event by one shot over Arnold Palmer and Charles Coe. Playing the par-3, 4, and 5 holes all under par that week, Player became the first international golfer to win the Masters Tournament.

Highs and Lows

The first hole has yielded four eagles in Masters Tournament history, the first by Frank Moore in 1940

"A drive that is long and straight, skirting a group of trees on the right will be in favorable position for the second. It is difficult to obtain par figures from any other position."

—ALISTER MACKENZIE, 1932

when it played at 400 yards. Roberto De Vicenzo carded a two here during the final round of the fateful 1968 tournament. Upon finishing his round De Vicenzo lost out on a playoff bid when it was discovered he had signed an incorrect scorecard. Two years later Takaaki Kono eagled the hole, and in 1987 Scott Verplank holed his approach to the first green from the fairway bunker.

Aside from Gary Player, three others have played the hole at 3-under par during the course of an entire Masters Tournament, including Curtis Strange twice (1984 and '92). Artie McNickle (1979) and José Maria Olazábal (1991) have also accomplished the feat.

Until recent Masters play the highest mark ever taken on the par-4 first hole was seven. But during play in the 1998 Masters, Olin Browne and Scott Simpson carded eights on the hole and three years later Billy Casper followed suit.

Nick Price hit his drive into the fairway bunker and bogeyed this hole to start his third round in the 1986 Masters. He followed with a record ten birdies over the remaining seventeen holes and established a new Masters Tournament single-round scoring mark of 63. "It is exhilarating to know I broke a record that stood for so long," Price said afterward. After an opening round 79, Price played the middle two rounds 12-under par to move into a four-way tie for second place. "It's the kind of course that when you get it going, you can really get it going," Price noted. But with a final-round 71, Price eventually finished in fifth place, his best showing to date in Masters play. His score was quickly overshadowed when Jack Nicklaus recorded a 65 the following day to win his sixth green jacket.

First Fairway, circa 1948 Late 1940s view from the tee box of the first fairway at the Augusta National Golf Club. (© Historic Golf Photos–Ron Watts Collection.)

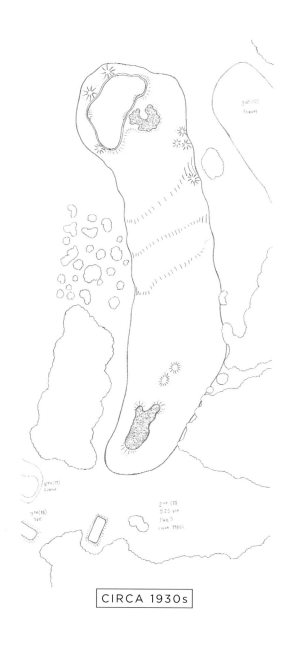

CIRCA 1930s

PRESENT

HOLE 2
The Longest Yards

MAJOR CHANGES

1946
Left-front greenside bunker added.

1953
Left-side putting surface expanded.

1966
Left-side fairway bunker relocated into the landing area.

1966
Right-front greenside bunker reduced in size.

1977
Left-front greenside bunker expanded.

1977
Tee box relocated to the right, adding 15 yards.

1996
Spectator mound to the back of the green pushed back.

1999
Fairway bunker moved more to the right.

1999
Tee box relocated 20–25 yards back.

Hole 2, circa 1934 When the Augusta National Golf Club first opened the course had just twenty-two bunkers, including this greenside bunker at the par-5 second hole. Another bunker was added to the front-left side of the putting surface in 1946. (Photo by Tony Sheehan. Courtesy of Joseph M. Lee III.)

par	5	PINK DOGWOOD
1934 yardage	525	
1959 yardage	555	
current yardage	575	
difficulty	16	

Shark Tale
Greg Norman reacts after scoring an eagle at the second hole during the 1989 tournament. Norman finished in a tie for third place with Ben Crenshaw. Nick Faldo won the event in a playoff with Scott Hoch. (Courtesy of Joe Dromsky Collection.)

"This is an interesting three shot hole down hill. Each shot will have to be placed with great accuracy if par figures are obtained. On the other hand, it is quite possible for a powerful and accurate player to reach the green in two shots."

—ALISTER MACKENZIE, 1932

Hole History

Once an easy two shots to the green for many golfers, this dogleg left has more teeth with the addition of a new back tee and repositioned fairway bunker for the 1999 Masters. These two changes injected a measure of strategy and once again it takes two excellent shots to reach the putting surface. Deep greenside bunkers guard both sides of a narrow, undulating putting surface. At 575 yards, it is the longest hole at the Augusta National and the lone par 5 yet to yield a double-eagle. The left greenside bunker was added in 1946 and twenty years later the bunker on the right side was cut back in size.

This first par 5 on the course is a good spot to start a rally. The putting surface is reachable in two, but for the golfer who comes up short, greenside bunkers await. Originally called the Woodbine hole, today it is known as Pink Dogwood for the trees that border its fairway.

Memorable Moments

After back-to-back second-place finishes, Ralph Guldahl rode the second hole to victory in the 1939 Masters. Guldahl played the hole at 5-under par that year en route to his winning score of 9-under par 279, one shot better than Sam Snead.

Second Scene The wide open fairway leading to the par-5 second hole as it appeared in 1948. Babe Ruth's backup on the New York Yankees, Sam Byrd, posted a record high ten at the hole the year this photo was taken. (© Historic Golf Photos – Ron Watts collection.)

"The 'alternate route' is again emphasized. The long hitter can reach home on his second shot, while the more timid souls can make their pars with safety-first tactics."

—*NEW YORK TIMES*, 1933

Highs and Lows

Aside from Guldahl, ten others have played the second hole at 5-under par for the week, including four former champions. Sam Snead (1942), Ben Hogan (1946), Tom Watson (1994), and Phil Mickelson (1998) accomplished the feat in years they did not win the event.

Though it is the longest hole on the course and the only par 5 yet to yield a double-eagle, the second hole has been the site of 165 eagles. Baseball player turned golf star Sammy Byrd had a not so pleasant memory of the second hole. Babe Ruth's backup for six seasons with the New York Yankees, Byrd later turned to a career in golf, where he won twenty-three tournaments as a professional. In 1948 Byrd posted a ten at the second, the highest score on this hole in Masters Tournament history. Red Smith of the New York Herald Tribune wrote of Byrd's antics, "He'd got in the woods there, clubbed a few rattlesnakes to death before getting out, and missed a three-footer for a nine." Byrd remarked, "After a while it got to be funny." Then after reflecting, he remarked, "Well, not really funny."

"It was one of our guiding principles in building the Augusta National that even our par fives should be reachable by two excellent shots. The possibility of using the downslope off the tee shot brings this long hole into this category. The contours of the fairway and the mounds at the top of the hill were constructed for the very purpose of aiding the player to make use of the slope in order to gain length. But to do so, he must drive accurately."

—BOBBY JONES, 1959

Second Scene, circa 1994
View of the second fairway and putting surface with the seventh green in the middle right of the photo. At 575 yards, the second hole is the longest test on the course. (Courtesy of Michael O'Byrne Photography.)

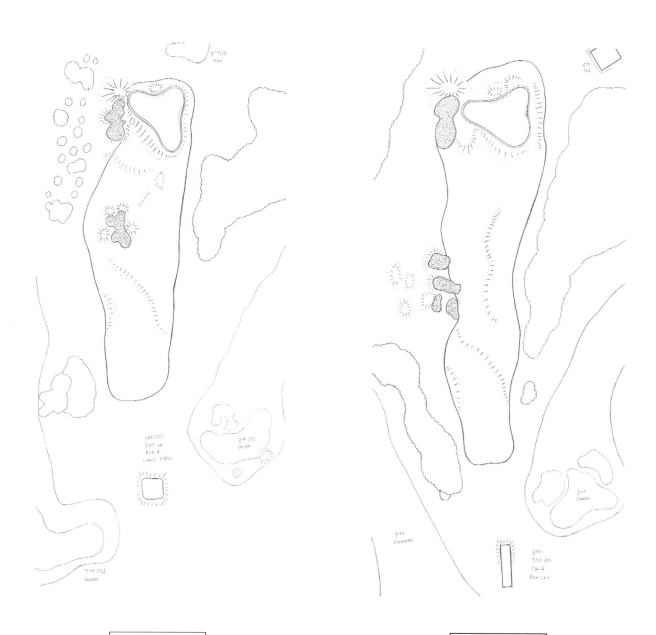

CIRCA 1930s

PRESENT

HOLE 3
MacKenzie's Best

Hole 3, circa 1934 Alister MacKenzie felt the third hole at Augusta National Golf Club was nearly perfect in design and it has undergone the least amount of change since the first Invitation Tournament. (Photo by Tony Sheehan. Courtesy of Joseph M. Lee III.)

MAJOR CHANGES

1953
Tee box moved to the right.

1982
Cluster of left-side fairway bunkers added.

par	4	
1934 yardage	350	
1959 yardage	355	**FLOWERING PEACH**
current yardage	350	
difficulty	14	

Third Green, circa 1948 The third hole plays the same distance it did when the first Augusta National Invitation Tournament was staged in 1934, but a cluster of fairway bunkers established in 1982 has added strategy to the tee shot. (© of Historic Golf Photos–Ron Watts Collection.)

"The second shot is the important shot here for the left-hand side of the green is narrow and the right-hand side wide, but in nine times out of ten the hole will be cut in the left-hand side."

—*NEW YORK TIMES*, 1933

Hole History

The shortest of the par 4s at the Augusta National, this hole measures the same distance it did when the first Augusta National Invitation Tournament (Masters) was played in 1934. MacKenzie felt this hole was nearly perfect in design, but if Clifford Roberts had his way another bunker would have been added in front of the green. Jones and MacKenzie were able to convince him otherwise. According to David Owen's book, *The Making of the Masters*, MacKenzie wrote to Roberts and stated, "I am delighted that Bob agrees that the [third] with the one trap is all right. This confirms my impression that Bob knows more about golf and its sound principles than any man I have ever come across.

No player in Masters history has dominated two holes back-to-back in the same tournament like Ken Venturi did at the second and third holes in 1960.

My own opinion is that a cross bunker would convert it into any ordinary stereotyped hole and would nullify all the subtleties of the undulations of the approach to which we gave so much time and thought."

The only notable change to this hole came in 1982 with the addition of four bunkers grouped to the left of the fairway. A carry of 280 yards off the tee is needed to clear the hazards.

It is better to be long than short on the approach shot or a golfer faces an uphill shot to a putting surface that slopes from right to left. The traditional final round left-side pin placement can be especially challenging as the green is narrow and guarded by a bunker.

Memorable Moments

No player in Masters history has dominated two holes back-to-back in the same tournament like Ken Venturi did at the second and third holes in 1960. During first-round action, Venturi carded eagle-birdie over the second and third holes en route to a front-nine 31. But he gave the shots back during a back-nine 42. Still, he followed with birdies over the two-hole stretch the final three days.

While Venturi played the two holes a combined 9-under par in 1960 it would not be enough to win the tournament. Venturi finished regulation play at 5-

"This green is situated on an interesting natural plateau. The left-hand side of the green is very narrow; whereas the right side is broad. It is easy for anyone to reach the wide portion of the green with their second shot but difficult to reach the narrow end where the pin will usually be placed."

—ALISTER MACKENZIE, 1932

"The green on the left is very shallow on the right side, it is very deep but slopes away from the player so that it is not easy to be certain of the exact location of the flag. The main problem presented by the second shot, which is normally played with a wedge or 8-iron, is to gauge the distance precisely. With the pin on the left, a second shot played either short or over leaves a very difficult pitch."

—BOBBY JONES, 1959

under par 283, one shot in back of Arnold Palmer who won his second green jacket. The *Augusta Chronicle* noted Venturi's "Greatness in defeat" and Sports Editor Johnny Hendrix included in his column mention of the "steady pulsating ovation Venturi received when introduced by Bob Jones." Jones remarked of Venturi's stellar play during the week: "I can understand the forty-two, but what I can't understand is how anybody could shoot thirty-one."

Between 1956 and 1960, Venturi finished second twice and also posted a third-place finish. In those events (1956, 1958, and 1960) Venturi was a combined four shots shy of forcing or taking part in playoffs for three green jackets.

It would be forty-three years before another golfer would match Venturi's 1960 performance of 3-3-3-3 at the third hole; K. J. Choi became the second golfer to do so during the 2003 tournament.

Highs and Lows
During the 1980 tournament, Douglas B. Clarke became the lone participant in Masters history to score an eight on this hole. In contrast, nine eagles have been produced at the third hole during Masters Tournament play, including a second-round eagle in 1985 by Curtis Strange. The shot sparked a dramatic turnabout in his play and inspired Strange to complete the final three rounds 12-under par. His second-round 65 was fifteen shots better than his opening-round score. Had he not posted an 80 during Thursday's first round, Strange would likely have coasted to a green jacket. Instead, he finished in a three-way tie for second place, two shots in back of that year's winner, Bernhard Langer.

Sock It to 'Em Arnold Palmer makes ready for historic happenings during the 1960 Masters, which he won by one shot. (© Historic Golf Photos–Ron Watts Collection.)

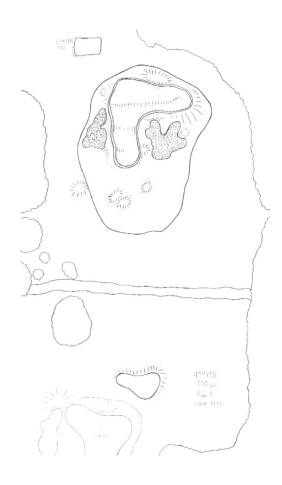

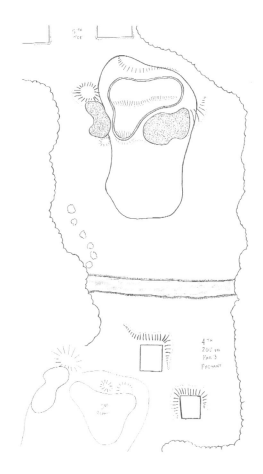

CIRCA 1930s

PRESENT

HOLE 4
Difficult Par 3

Hole 4, circa 1934 A second tee box was added to the fourth hole prior to the 1964 tournament. The original tee designed by Alister MacKenzie is still utilized one day each tournament. (Photo by Tony Sheehan. Courtesy of Joseph M. Lee III.)

MAJOR CHANGES

1964
Second tee box installed back and right.

par	3	
1934 yardage	190	
1959 yardage	220	
current yardage	205	
difficulty	3	

FLOWERING CRAB APPLE

Famous Fourth View of the par-3 fourth hole, tee to green in the late 1940s. (© Historic Golf Photos–Ron Watts Collection.)

"This is a very similar hole to the famous Eleventh (Eden) at St. Andrews. There have been scores of attempted copies of this famous hole but there is none that has the charm and thrills of the original. Most copies are failures because of the absence of the subtle and severe slopes which create the excitement of the original hole, and also because the turf is usually so soft that any kind of a sloppy pitch will stop. Previous failures, followed by, comparatively speaking, increasing successes may have given us sufficient experience to warrant us in hoping that here at last we may have constructed a hole that will compare favorably with the original."

—ALISTER MACKENZIE, 1932

Hole History

At 205 yards, the fourth hole remains the longest and most difficult par 3 at the Augusta National. A tee box at the fourth hole that was in play during the first Invitation Tournament is still utilized once during each tournament. Greenside bunkers guard the left and front-right sides of the long, contoured putting surface that slopes from back to front. Coupled with swirling winds, it all adds up to the third-hardest hole in Masters Tournament history. Errors here can be magnified as there is little time to regroup; the following fifth hole is ranked as the fifth most difficult. Not only are the AugustaNational's fourth and fifth holes the toughest back-to-back holes in Masters history, they represent the second-toughest stretch on the course next to holes ten through twelve. Early in the Augusta National's existence, this was known as the Palm Hole for trees that were prevalent on the course there. Bamboo shoots line the right side of the hole along Berckmans Road and give the hole a fittingly exotic feel.

The thickly planted bamboo shoots also serve as a sound barrier from Berckmans Road, which runs the length of the hole.

Bamboo Buddies, circa 1985
Arnold Palmer makes ready to hit from the bamboo shoots that line the Augusta National Golf Club. Bamboo is prevalent along the fourth and fifth holes off Berckmans Road and along Washington Road as a border to the Par-3 Course. (Courtesy of Joe Dromsky Collection.)

Memorable Moments

Jeff Sluman's ace with a 4-iron from 213 yards in 1992 marks the only hole-in-one here in Masters Tournament history. The achievement aided Sluman in his share of the first- round lead and gave him momentum for an eventual fourth-place finish that year.

Course codesigner Bobby Jones and David Toms are the only two golfers in Masters history to birdie the hole in three rounds during the same tournament.

Highs and Lows

While Jeff Sluman's is the only hole-in-one at the fourth hole, four players have posted quadruple bogey sevens there: Dave Eichelberger in 1965, Jim Colbert in 1972, Nathaniel Crosby during the 1982 event, and Doug Ford in the 2000 Masters Tournament.

Par-3 Four, circa 1994 The cornerstone on the front nine of the Augusta National Golf Club, the fourth hole plays as one of the toughest on the course. (Courtesy of Michael O'Byrne Photography.)

"This hole can be varied a great deal, depending upon the use of the back tee or the rear portion of the forward tee. At tournament time there is very often a heavy wind on this hole directly against or quartering off the right. The back tee is somewhat elevated so that the shot is exposed to the violence of any wind which may be blowing. On certain days the wind will place many players in the left-hand bunker or beyond."

—BOBBY JONES, 1959

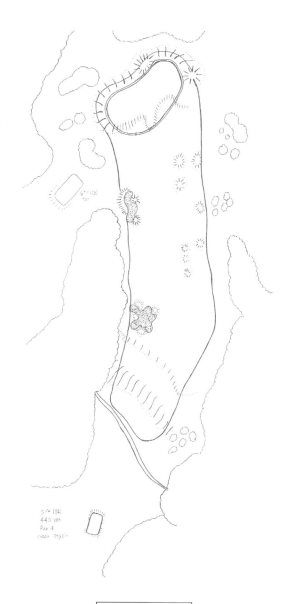

CIRCA 1930s

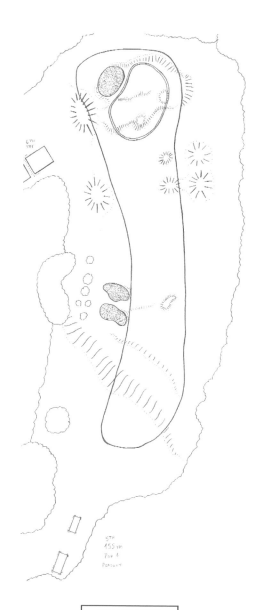

PRESENT

HOLE 5
Four Is a Good Score

Hole 5, circa 1934 Early photo of the fifth hole where a back-left greenside bunker was constructed in 1956. The two-tiered putting surface is riddled with signature MacKenzie undulations that increase the difficulty of the hole. (Photo by Tony Sheehan. Courtesy of Joseph M. Lee III.)

MAJOR CHANGES

1953
Tee extended forward up 10 yards.

1956
Back-left greenside bunker established.

1964
Mounds added to the right-side fairway in front of the putting surface.

1967
Left greenside mound expanded.

1972
Apron of putting surface lengthened.

2003
Tee moved back and fairway bunkers extended 80 yards toward the putting surface.

2003
Bunkers and fairway shifted to the right to increase the dogleg.

		MAGNOLIA
par	4	
1934 yardage	440	
1959 yardage	450	
current yardage	455	
difficulty	5	

Fifth Fairway, circa 1948 An early glimpse of the fifth fairway from the tee. Major changes to the hole put in place for the 2004 tournament included moving the left-side fairway bunkers 80 yards closer to the hole. (© Historic Golf Photos–Ron Watts Collection.)

"This is a similar type of hole to the famous Seventeenth, the Road Hole at St. Andrews. A group of trees forms a corner of the dogleg instead of the station masters garden and the green itself is situated on a similar plateau to its prototype."

—ALISTER MACKENZIE, 1932

"The proper line here is, as closely possible, past the bunker on the left side of the fairway. The bunker and the woods to the left of it usually represent dire disaster. Players lacking the confidence to play along the dangerous line sometimes become overcautious and play down the right side of the fairway. From this side the second shot becomes much longer and far more difficult. With the green's surface in proper condition, the second shot must be dropped short and allowed to run up."

—BOBBY JONES, 1959

Hole History

Sandwiched between a pair of par-3 tests, the fifth hole is the hardest par 4 on the front side. This uphill, dogleg left was in recent years considered an easy driving hole, but it is now fraught with challenge. With additional yardage in length and the left-side fairway bunkers repositioned closer to the green for the 2003 tournament, it now takes a drive with 315 yards of carry to clear the hazards. The putting surface slopes to the front and features dramatic undulations. A back-left bunker collects shots hit long, making it that much harder to get approach shots close. Feeling that the green was challenging enough, Jones did not initially agree that fairway bunkers were needed on the hole.

When the fifth-hole fairway was redressed with topsoil in 1962, club cofounder Clifford Roberts utilized a unique method to test its completion. To ensure the fairway had no bumps, course superintendent John Graves was instructed to ride its length at maximum speed in a golf cart.

Memorable Moments

It was on the fifth hole in 1995 that Jack Nicklaus scored eagles during the first and third rounds, resulting in a record-tying 3-under par for the hole for the week. Nicklaus remains the only golfer in Masters history to register two eagles on a par-4 hole in the same tournament, let alone the same hole. Nicklaus has scored more eagles than any participant in Masters history with twenty-four, including three at par-4 holes.

While Nicklaus' eagle run in 1995 led him to play the hole at 3-under par for the week, seven others have played the hole at that pace during the course of one tournament.

Highs and Lows

Between 1957 and 1964 came the only eights produced at the hole; Bill Campbell and Sam Parks in 1957, Chick Harbert during the 1960 tournament, and Jerry Barber in 1964. In contrast, the hole did not yield an eagle until 1974, a full forty years after the tournament's inception. During the past thirty years of competition, seven additional eagles have been carded at the fifth hole, including the two by Nicklaus in 1995. Scott Hoch recorded a two at the hole in 1983 and Curtis Strange did it in 1987. The 2000 Masters saw two more eagles; one each by Colin Montgomerie and Gabriel Hjertstedt. Rich Beem added his name to the list in 2003.

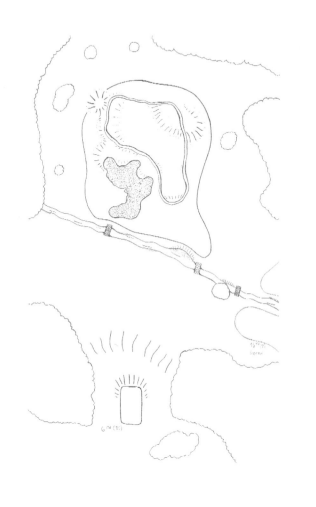

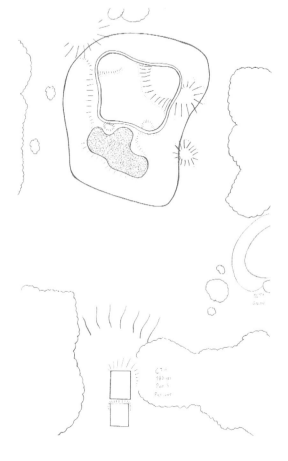

CIRCA 1930s

PRESENT

HOLE 6
Short, but Not Sweet

Scenic Sixth The tributary to Rae's Creek that fronted the sixth green was converted into a pond in the mid-1950s, but by decade's end was covered over. The sixth is the only hole at the Augusta National Golf Club that plays shorter than it did during the 1934 tournament. (Courtesy of Western Golf Association.)

MAJOR CHANGES

1959
Pond in front of green filled in.

1975
Tee box reconstructed.

par	3	
1934 yardage	185	
1959 yardage	190	JUNIPER
current yardage	180	
difficulty	13	

Scenic Sixth The sixth hole as it looked when amateur Billy Joe Patton scored a hole-in-one during the 1954 Masters Tournament. Patton finished regulation play one shot back of Ben Hogan and eventual playoff winner Sam Snead. (© Historic Golf Photos–Ron Watts Collection.)

"This is similar to the Redan Hole at North Berwick (Scotland), but here, owing to its extreme visibility, lie of the land, and beauty of the surroundings, we have no doubt that we have constructed a much more attractive hole than the original Redan."

—ALISTER MACKENZIE, 1932

While the par-3 fourth and twelfth holes mark the Augusta National's farthest borders, the sixth and sixteenth holes come together to form a natural amphitheater, which is a favorite among patrons.

Hole History

The sixth marks the lone hole on the course that actually plays shorter than it did for the first Invitation Tournament in 1934. The easiest of the par-3 holes over the course of Masters Tournament history, it features an elevated tee and a large two-tier putting surface. Coupled with severe side slope and a dramatic change in elevation from front to back, putting on this green is another challenge. A lone greenside bunker guards the front-left side of the putting surface. While the par-3 fourth and twelfth holes mark the Augusta National's farthest borders, the sixth and sixteenth holes come together to form a natural amphitheater, which is a favorite among patrons. In early Tournament history, the same tributary of Rae's Creek that winds along the thirteenth hole continued in front of the sixth hole. In 1955 the creek was made into a pond and four years later was covered over completely.

Memorable Moments

Amateur Billy Joe Patton's ace during the final round of the 1954 tournament is most memorable in that it helped this fan favorite regain the top spot on the Sunday leaderboard, the place he occupied after the first two rounds. A relatively unknown Walker Cup team alternate, Patton ignited the galleries and made his mark on Masters history. He eventually finished the tournament one shot back of Sam Snead and Ben Hogan.

The two par 5s on the back side, the two easiest scoring holes in Masters history, would prove to be his undoing. At thirteen, Patton's second shot hit the creek in front of the green, and after a penalty shot and poor approach, he carded a seven. Two holes later, his approach shot found the water in front of the fifteenth green and he bogeyed the hole. Playing conservatively on those two holes would have assured Patton a green jacket. Instead, the two "birdie" holes at Augusta National had cost him three shots. When he added up his scorecard that fateful Sunday afternoon, Patton's total was just one shot in back of Sam Snead and Ben Hogan. Undeterred, Patton would later say, "I didn't come to play safe."

Snead won the following day's playoff and green jacket, while Patton extended his stay in Augusta at the invitation of President Dwight D. Eisenhower. The

Sixth Summit circa 1994 The view from the putting surface of the 6th hole looking back toward the elevated tee box at the Augusta National Golf Club. (Courtesy Michael O'Byrne Photography)

amateur's style of play not only captured the imagination of the public, but also caught the eye of the president, with whom Patton played golf later that week. The Snead-Hogan playoff pushed back the start of the president's spring stay at the Augusta National by one day that year.

Highs and Lows

In addition to Billy Joe Patton's hole in one in 1954, three other Masters competitors have scored aces on the hole. The aces by Patton and Leland Gibson have something in common in that both feats were accomplished in 1954. In 1972, Charles Coody used a 5-iron to travel the 190 yards to the cup. Fifty years after the first aces at the hole, Chris DiMarco scored a hole in one at the sixth hole in 2004.

Eight Masters competitors have played the sixth hole at 3-under par for the week, including Gay Brewer, whose play at the hole helped buoy his victory in 1967. Tom Weiskopf's 3-under par effort at this par 3 during the epic 1975 Masters battle helped bring him to within one shot of Jack Nicklaus.

The highest score posted at the hole during Masters Tournaments (7) came at the hands of Masters champions—José Maria Olazábal in his prime in 1991, and Arnold Palmer in the latter stages of his career in 1997.

Patton Pride Billy Joe Patton receives low amateur honors from Bobby Jones for his performance in the 1954 Masters. Patton lost out on a playoff berth with Ben Hogan and eventual winner Sam Snead by one shot. (© Historic Golf Photos–Ron Watts Collection.)

"The early difficult pin area here is formed by the plateau at the back-right corner. To land upon and hold this plateau, the shot must be very accurately struck. With the ball either short of this area or to the left, the first putt is extremely difficult. The front of the green immediately behind the bunker is the easiest location. Back of this, the side slope is severe."

—BOBBY JONES, 1959

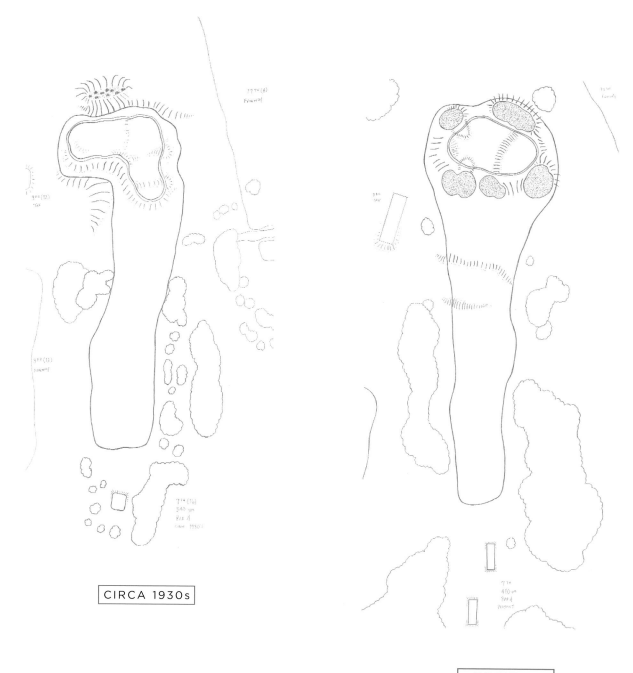

CIRCA 1930s

PRESENT

HOLE 7
Maxwell's Major Changes

Hole 7, circa 1934 Early view of the unguarded seventh hole putting surface. At the suggestion of 1934 and 1936 champion Horton Smith, the hole was redesigned by MacKenzie associate Perry Maxwell to include three greenside bunkers. The green is now surrounded by five bunkers. (Photo by Tony Sheehan. Courtesy of Joseph M. Lee III.)

MAJOR CHANGES

1938
Green rebuilt and bunkers added to front.

1951
Tee box extended forward.

1951
Putting surface elevated and bunkers added.

1951
Back bunkers added.

2002
Tee box relocated 40–45 yards back.

2002
Section of fairway landing area regraded.

par	4	
1934 yardage	340	
1959 yardage	365	PAMPAS
current yardage	410	
difficulty	12	

Seventh Side Side view of the well-guarded seventh green at the Augusta National Golf Club as it appeared in 1948. A pair of backside bunkers were added in 1951. (© Historic Golf Photos–Ron Watts Collection.)

"This hole is similar in character to the Eighteenth Hole at St. Andrews, Scotland. There is a deep hollow at the front of the green which it is necessary to attack at the correct angle for par figures to be obtained. At this hole it will also be desirable to play a run-up shot as it will be exceedingly difficult to retain a pitch in the usual position of the flag."

—ALISTER MACKENZIE, 1932

Major changes to the course for the 2002 Masters Tournament called for the seventh tee to be moved back 45 yards and the left-side tree line extended.

Hole History

Alister MacKenzie and Bobby Jones originally designed the Augusta National with thirty-six bunkers, but upon MacKenzie's advice the duo cut the total back to twenty-two. Still, Bobby Jones felt the Augusta National was the best inland course in America. When the course first opened, the seventh, fifteenth, and seventeenth holes all played without bunkers. By 1938 the seventh green was fronted by three bunkers and today it is surrounded by five such hazards. While the fourteenth hole currently has no bunkers, through 1951 it featured a fairway bunker.

Once considered among the weaker holes at the Augusta National, the seventh is now one of the toughest. Several major modifications have been made to the hole during the course of Masters history. Originally designed by MacKenzie and Jones to be a played as a drive and pitch, the strategy was altered when technology made it possible for golfers to hit their drives near the putting surface.

Acting on the suggestion of 1934 and '36 champion Horton Smith, the seventh hole was rebuilt in 1938 to include front greenside bunkers. In addition, MacKenzie associate Perry Maxwell relocated and elevated the multicontoured green. In 1951, two more bunkers were added to the back of the putting surface.

For the next half-century the hole was secure, until the next wave of technology impacted the game.

Major changes to the course for the 2002 Masters Tournament called for the seventh tee to be moved back 45 yards and the left-side tree line extended. Originally known as the Cedar hole, the pampas trees planted along the left side in 1959 have matured and grown to just over 30 yards apart from those on the opposite side of the fairway, providing golfers with a challenging narrow chute to aim for. A blind second shot to this elevated, shallow, well-guarded putting surface makes for testy approach shots. Adding to the challenge, the seventh green is divided in two with an overall front-to-back slope.

Memorable Moments

Though he did not win the tournament in 1998, fifty-eight-year-old Jack Nicklaus saved maybe his best performance for Sunday's final round. With back-to-back birdies at the sixth and seventh holes—his third and fourth on the front side—Nicklaus pulled to within two shots of leaders José Maria Olazábal and Mark O'Meara. Thirty-five years removed from his first Masters victory in 1963, Nicklaus' exploits elicited thunderous roars from the gallery, those reserved only for Sunday play, and Nicklaus, at Augusta.

"The tee shot on this hole becomes tighter year by year as the pine trees on either side of the fairway continue to spread. Length is not a premium here, but the narrow fairway seems to have an added impact because it suddenly confronts the player when he has become accustomed to the broad expanses of the preceding hole. The green is quite wide, but also very shallow."

—BOBBY JONES, 1959

During first-round play in the 1996 Masters, Greg Norman played the first six holes at even par. Then he followed with a 35-foot birdie putt at the seventh hole that changed everything. Before the day was out, Norman rolled in eight more birdies, an effort that tied him with Nick Price's 63 in the third round of the 1986 Masters for course-record honors. More importantly, it gave Norman the tournament lead, which he maintained until a final-round collapse that gave way to Nick Faldo, who captured his third Masters victory.

In the third round of the 1999 Masters, Steve Pate posted the first of seven consecutive birdies beginning at the seventh hole. Pate finished with a round of 65 that day and in a tie for fourth place in the tournament. Johnny Miller's third round in the classic 1975 Masters included a string of six consecutive birdies that concluded with a long birdie putt from off the green at the seventh hole.

Highs and Lows

Three golfers have posted 3-3-3-3 at the hole during the Masters Tournament and each finished no farther back than third place overall. Sam Snead accomplished the feat in 1957 when he was runner-up to Jimmy Demaret. Thirty-seven years later, Larry Mize posted a birdie at the seventh hole each day en route to a third-place finish behind José Maria Olazábal. David Duval began a new century of Masters golf history at the seventh hole with his birdie binge during a second-place finish to Tiger Woods in 2001.

The seventh hole has yielded eight eagles throughout Masters history. All eight eagles were recorded by golfers who have won major championships. Ernie Els accomplished the feat twice (1997 and 2003). Ben Curtis, 2003 British Open champion, followed with an eagle at the hole in 2004. Of the remaining five golfers to eagle the hole, four are former Masters champions, including Jack Nicklaus (1976), Tommy Aaron (1986), Fuzzy Zoeller (1992), and Larry Mize (1999), all during years they did not win the tournament. Dick Mayer, 1957 U.S. Open winner, was first to eagle the hole during the 1955 Masters.

DeWitt Weaver (1972) and Richard L. von Tacky Jr. (1981) share the distinction of being the lone Masters competitors to post eights on their scorecards after playing the hole. In the first round of the 1972 tournament, Charles Coody left the seventh hole with jumbled emotions. In defense of his 1971 Masters title, Coody scored a hole in one at the sixth hole and followed with a near-record seven at the seventh hole.

Seventh Heaven? circa 1994 Tee to green at the par-4 seventh hole. The hole was lengthened by 45 yards prior to the 2002 tournament. (Courtesy of Michael O'Byrne Photography.)

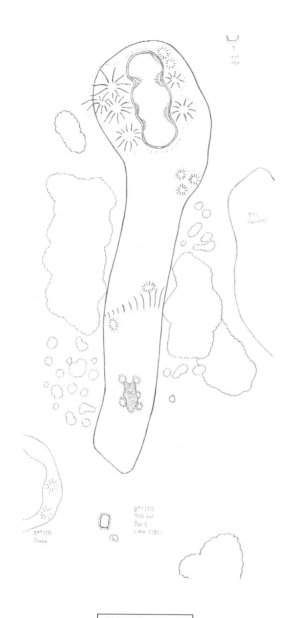

CIRCA 1930s

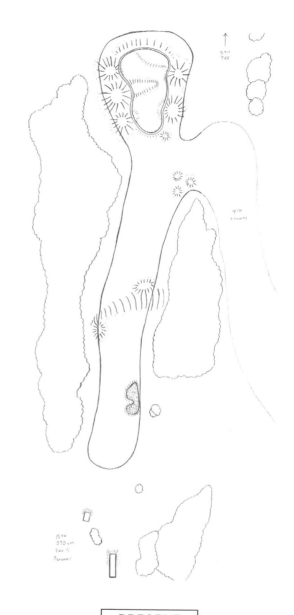

PRESENT

HOLE 8
Uphill Battle

Hole 8, circa 1934 Alister MacKenzie's creative use of mounds is never more evident than at the well-guarded par-5 eighth hole. The mounds were more cost-effective than bunkers and were part of MacKenzie's scheme of aesthetics and strategy. (Photo by Tony Sheehan. Courtesy of Joseph M. Lee III.)

MAJOR CHANGES

1956
Putting surface redesigned.

1957
Putting surface redesigned and mounds guarding left side of green removed.

1957
Right-side fairway bunker moved right.

1964
Tee box moved back and right.

1979
Putting surface rebuilt to reflect MacKenzie's original specifications and left greenside mounds replaced.

2002
Right-side fairway bunker almost doubled in size.

2002
Tee box relocated 15–20 yards back and right.

par	5
1934 yardage	500
1959 yardage	530
current yardage	570
difficulty	15

YELLOW JASMINE

Eighth Green Right-rear view of the original eighth hole prior to removal of mounds on the far side of the putting surface in 1957. Two-time Masters champion Byron Nelson oversaw reconstruction of the mounds in 1979. (© Historic Golf Photos–Ron Watts Collection.)

"This hole is a three shot hole up hill. The green is in a punch bowl surrounded by large hillocks nine to twelve feet high. It is completely visible for the third shot and a player who is sufficiently long to get up in two will be able to define the position of the green owing to the size of the surrounding hillock. It may be compared to the Seventeenth Green at Muirfield [Edinburgh, Scotland.]"

—ALISTER MACKENZIE, 1932

During the memorable 1986 Masters, the final-round drama included back–to-back eagles at the eighth hole by Tom Kite and Seve Ballesteros, the only two eagles there during the entire tournament.

Hole History

Five yards shorter than the par-5 second hole, the eighth hole with its uphill design plays as the longest on the course. The most difficult of four par 5s at the Augusta National, the eighth marks the first of three consecutive holes featuring extreme elevation changes.

In 1956, changes to the green resulted in an poorly shaped putting surface and harsh words from Bobby Jones. The new green resembled a huge pancake at the end of the fairway. Jones disliked the work so much he remarked to club cofounder Clifford Roberts that "they were wrecking the course." For the 1956 Masters Tournament, a sign displayed near the green hinted the work was not permanent. Architect George Cobb was ushered in at the conclusion of that year's tournament to rebuild the green to more conventional standards.

The earlier message to Roberts apparently fell on deaf ears, because one year later he tinkered with the eighth hole again. To provide a better view of the putting surface for patrons, Roberts had "MacKenzie's mounds" removed from the left side of the green for the 1957 tournament. This change was in force through the 1978 Masters, after which Byron Nelson supervised the mound's return.

Changes for the 2002 Masters included lengthening the hole 20 yards and a major increase in the size of the right-side fairway bunker. A repositioned tee box brings the bunker more into play and a drive with 315 yards of carry is now mandatory to clear the hazard. Since 1979, the mounds that MacKenzie originally designed to guard the left side of the green are back in play.

Memorable Moments

During the exciting 1986 Masters, the final-round drama included back–to-back eagles at the eighth hole by Tom Kite and Seve Ballesteros, the only two eagles there during the entire tournament. Going first, Kite used a sand wedge to hole his shot from 80 yards as the gallery erupted. Ballesteros answered moments later by sinking his pitch shot from 50 yards away. Again the gallery thundered from high atop the hill at the eighth. Playing two groups ahead of the Kite-Ballesteros pairing that day, Jack Nicklaus backed off his birdie putt on the ninth green twice in response to the roars.

"This is another par five which can be reached under normal conditions with two fine shots. Here again, although the line is not directly over the bunker, it is well to hit the tee shot with sufficient power to make the carry. It is important that the ball be kept a bit to the right of center of the fairway so that the second shot may be played through the saddle formed by the mounds at the top of the hill and so directly toward the green. Should he play left to avoid the bunker, the player must skirt the trees on the left with his second shot in order to get very near the green."

—BOBBY JONES, 1959

With Greg Norman also in the hunt and awaiting his approach from the ninth fairway, Nicklaus settled in and made his putt. The gallery surrounding the ninth hole sent out a roar of its own as if to mark the start of the greatest back-nine Sunday classic in Masters history.

Highs and Lows

No one in Masters history has played the eighth hole better than Bruce Devlin during the 1967 Masters. Devlin's first round included an approach shot at the eighth hole with a 4-wood from 248 yards out. When the shot fell into the cup Devlin recorded the only double-eagle ever recorded at the hole and just the second in Masters history. Though he played the eighth hole at 6-under par for the week, he finished the tournament at 2-over par, ten shots in back of Gay Brewer.

During the second Invitation Tournament in 1935, Frank Walsh found out just how hard playing the hole with mounds intact could be, as he recorded a record high twelve on his scorecard.

Surround Mounds, circa 1994 The use of mounds more than makes up for the lack of bunkers at this green. "MacKenzie's mounds" to the left side of the putting surface were removed in 1957 and rebuilt in 1979 to his original specifications. (Courtesy of Michael O'Byrne Photography.)

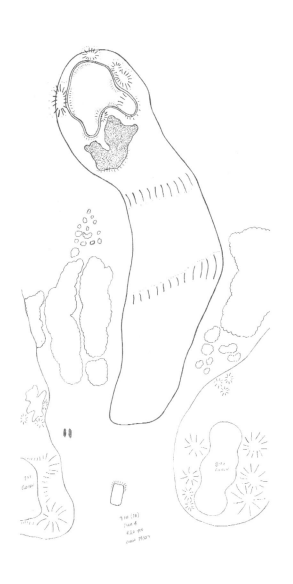

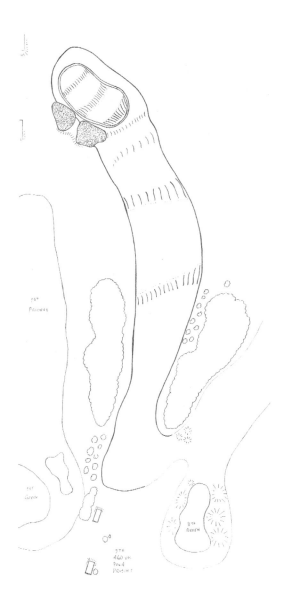

CIRCA 1930s

PRESENT

HOLE 9
Roller Coaster

Hole 9, circa 1934 Early view of the ninth hole where the putting surface was guarded by a lone bunker that ran the length of the green. This was the closing hole for the inaugural Augusta National Invitation Tournament. (Photo by Tony Sheehan. Courtesy of Joseph M. Lee III.)

MAJOR CHANGES

1958
Spectator mounds to the back and right of putting surface established.

1972
Left greenside mound expanded.

1973
Tee box relocated 26 yards back and right.

2002
Tee box moved back 25–30 yards.

par	4	
1934 yardage	420	
1959 yardage	420	
current yardage	460	
difficulty	11	

CAROLINA CHERRY

Ninth, circa 1950s Distant view of the ninth green from the opening between the eighth and ninth fairways at the Augusta National Golf Club. (Courtesy of Summerville Photo.)

"This hole is a hole of the Cape type played slightly downhill. A long straight drive to the right will give an easy second to the green."

—ALISTER MACKENZIE, 1932

In 1978 Gary Player began one of the great charges in Masters history at the ninth hole.

Hole History

This dogleg par 4 was the closing hole for the first Augusta National Invitation Tournament in 1934, won by Horton Smith by one shot over Craig Wood. That fall, the nines were reversed permanently. Alister MacKenzie originally designed the hole to play 420 yards, but with the impact of technology on golf equipment, competitors began driving their tee shots to a level area at the bottom of the hill that leads back up to an elevated green. Since the fairway drops off nearly 50 feet before rising back to the green, it is more advantageous to play an approach shot from the flat turf at the bottom of the hill rather than from a slightly downhill stance to the sloping putting surface that awaits. In 1952 the ninth hole was remeasured to play 10 yards shorter; in 1973 it was lengthened 26 yards; and in 1981 it was shortened again by 5 yards. For the 2002 tournament the tee box was moved back 25 yards to the 460 yards it now plays. Extra pine trees were added to the right side of the fairway, where the hole once opened up to allow a slightly longer but easier angle to the green. Approach shots played from the right side also provide a safer route to the three-tiered putting surface protected by left greenside bunkers.

Memorable Moments

In 1978 Gary Player began one of the great charges in Masters history at the ninth hole. Birdies over seven of the final ten holes enabled Player to shoot a final-round 64 and win the tournament by one shot over

Ninth Green Approach to the ninth hole as it appeared in 1948. The ditch to the far left continued across the first fairway and was covered over in 1951. (© Historic Golf Photos–Ron Watts Collection.)

Rod Funseth, Hubert Green, and Tom Watson. The victory marked Player's third and final Masters title.

Alister MacKenzie noted in his writings, "Some of the most spectacular shots I have ever seen have been around, over or through narrow gaps in trees." Two of the best shots on this hole came from the wooded area lining the left side of the fairway and certainly fit

Front-Nine Finale The ninth green as it appeared during the 1990 Masters Tournament won by Nick Faldo. In 1954, amateur Billy Joe Patton became the only participant in tournament history to record 3-3-3-3 at the hole. (Courtesy of Joe Dromsky Collection.)

"This is a slight dogleg to the left which invites the player to skirt the trees on the left side. Under normal circumstances, a long drive straight down the middle will give the best result since it will reach a reasonable flat area and provide an open shot for at least half the green. The hole opens up more and more as the drive is played to the right, but the distance becomes longer."

—BOBBY JONES, 1959

MacKenzie's description. The first was struck by Gary Player on the way to his first Masters win in 1961, and the second by Tiger Woods during the second round of his first win in 1997. Both shots saved par at this hole, saved one shot for each golfer, and proved historic in the overall scheme. Looking to take the short route to the bottom of the hill, Player's tee shot found the trees lining the left side of the fairway. That left him with an obstructed second shot to the green. Pitching out to the bottom of the hill fronting the green would be the most likely option. It was an option Player did not choose and his gamble paid off nicely. Instead, he hooked a second shot out of the woods and through the green, where he promptly got up and down for a classic par. The shot saved Player one shot in a tournament he won by a single shot over Arnold Palmer and Charles Coe. Taking a similar approach to Player's thirty-six years later, Tiger's gamble netted a slightly different spot in Masters history.

In 1986, Gary Player (Masters champion in 1961, 1974, and1978) commented on the course changes at the ninth and eighteenth holes: "I think they've possibly made a change for the better; however, I don't like to see them change this golf course, because this is like a Mona Lisa. Maybe you could go to the Mona Lisa and make little changes, but this has stood the test all throughout the years, and we've had all these players play it. I don't like to see them change this golf course. It's too great to go in and change."

Highs and Lows

Billy Joe Patton produced the best showing at the ninth hole in Masters history during the 1954 tournament. Patton's impressive 3-3-3-3 streak brought him to within one shot of taking part in the playoff with Ben Hogan and eventual champion Sam Snead. Patton gave back three of the four shots he earned at the ninth when he hit into water at both the thirteenth and fifteenth holes during final-round play.

Just four eagles have been produced at the ninth hole during the Masters Tournament, the first by Earl Stewart Jr. in the 1954 tournament, the same year that Billy Joe Patton birdied the hole all four days. Curtis Strange eagled the ninth in 1980, Steve Jones in 1991, and Danny Green during the 2000 Masters.

Jack Selby (1948) and Richard Davies (1963) have recorded the highest scores at the ninth, each taking eight shots to hole out.

Out of the Woods

The ninth hole at Augusta National Golf Club is a roller-coaster, dogleg left that requires a slight draw to set up the ideal approach shot to a severely sloped patch of green. A well-placed tee shot splits the center of a long chute bordered by tall pines on each side, before gently rolling to the bottom-right side of the fairway. A feat much easier said than done. Just ask Tiger Woods, whose early history at the ninth borders somewhere between ecstasy and agony. While this can be said for just about every hole at the Augusta National, nine is special in that it marks the halfway point in a golfer's round and many times proves a harbinger of things to come. It is here where golfers mentally make ready for the back nine and Amen Corner. Navigating the tee shot at nine may likely be the easy part. What remains can be even more intimidating: a mid- or short-iron shot to a sloped and elevated putting surface guarded by bunkers on the left and April breezes over all.

Chances are you've seen highlights of well-placed approach shots and putts alike coming within inches of the cup at number nine, only to see an extra half turn result in golf balls rolling far from a slanted tabletop green to an awaiting fairway. Nowhere on the course is the risk-reward factor greater than at number nine. A chance gust of wind, an extra half-turn of a Titleist on this severely sloping surface, and a birdie attempt comes up double bogey.

In 1997, Tiger Woods nearly shot himself out of the tournament with an opening-round 40 on the front nine. A 30 over the closing nine holes, however, brought Tiger to within three shots of the lead. Through eight holes on Friday, Woods had taken thirty shots to remain among the leaders. But in his zeal to reach the crosswalk at the bottom of the hill that leaves an easy approach, Tiger risked playing too far left along the tree line that borders the ninth fairway. Tiger's tee shot was followed by a faint "fore" and the unmistakable sound of golf ball against pine tree. It's not a pretty sound, but a sound you come to appreciate in Augusta nonetheless. A split second later a Titleist golf ball descended into a small clearing between the first and ninth fairways, surrounded by tall pines.

Moments later, a throng of patrons, gallery guards, and cameramen converged on the scene. Tiger's caddie at the time, Mike "Fluff" Cowan, strolled up to the clearing first, then Woods. Tiger was beside himself at the outcome and let out a short, high-pitched yelp in disbelief, like someone had just punched him in the stomach. Then in another instant Tiger's demeanor transformed into a focused, trance-like state. As he stared down his next shot, Tiger went from negative to positive and turned misfortune into opportunity in the blink of an eye. Most golfers would have taken their poison, pitched to the center of the fairway, and let the side-hill roll take the ball to the awaiting crosswalk at the bottom of the hill. Still a chance at par from there, not the best chance, but one I'm convinced most golfers in the field that day would have taken. From where he stood he could not even see the elevated, sloped putting surface that lay ahead. Par would feel like birdie from where his golf ball was situated. But in order to do so, Tiger would have to circumvent the trees to the center of the fairway, bend his golf ball 90 degrees, and still have enough on it to go another 175 yards—uphill. That's some imagination, Tiger!

It is the equivalent of a baseball player hitting a ball back up the middle past the pitcher's mound, then getting it to turn on a dime and hit third base. Got that shot in your bag, Tiger? That's the approach shot Tiger treated the gallery to and played it to perfection. Tiger got his golf ball airborne quickly, skirted the trees, turned hard, and—gone. When pressed for comments about the ninth hole by the media after his round, Tiger responded that he "duck-hooked it off the tee" and "duck-hooked another one because I had to." His response to what the (large) galleries were doing for him was even more humorous as Tiger was quick to note: "One, they're stopping a couple of my shots." Indeed.

On any given Friday, Tiger's second duck-hook would likely have gone an additional 50 yards. But this was Masters Friday and that assuredly meant a big gallery surrounding the ninth green, straining for a glimpse of Tiger's destiny. The gallery never saw it coming, never even saw him hit the golf ball. In the matter of an instant a golf ball appeared from nowhere, ricocheted off an unsuspecting patron, and bounced back toward the green. Two putt. Par. The kind of shot Bobby Jones may have envisioned when he reversed the nines and made this the closing hole of the first Masters Tournament in 1934.

Was Tiger's shot that Friday afternoon in 1997 a stroke of genius or lucky break? Depends on how you look at it. *Sports Illustrated* featured Tiger's miracle golf shot as a foldout in the following week's edition, and rightfully so. It was likely the best-played shot the entire week, and one that turned the tide en route to a Masters championship, by the man who broke the tournament scoring record by one shot; the shot produced from jail at number nine on Friday, not at eighteen on Sunday.

The Turn

First
ANNUAL
INVITATION
TOURNAMENT

Augusta
NATIONAL
GOLF
CLUB

MARCH - 22 · 23 - 24 - 25
AUGUSTA GEORGIA

The Augusta National Invitation Tournament

From 1934 through 1938, Bobby Jones' annual golf event in Augusta was officially known as the Augusta National Invitation Tournament. During those five years the title Clifford Roberts originally favored for the event, "The Masters," caught on with the media. By 1939 the event was officially designated as the Masters Tournament.

The first Augusta National Invitation Tournament Program in 1934 included articles on the old Fruitlands Nurseries and the new golf course, along with pictures of the grounds and key members of the club. It also included descriptions of each hole and the following article written by Alister MacKenzie, in which Roberts requested that Jones' contributions be highlighted.

The Augusta National Golf Club

A DESCRIPTION BY THE LATE DR. ALISTER MACKENZIE

(Written during the final stages of the construction period)

"In writing a description of the course I designed at Augusta, Georgia, for the Augusta National Golf Club, I want to emphasize the importance of the part played by Bobby Jones in working out the plans. Bobby is not only the President of the Club, but is the active leader in all matters pertaining to designing, construction and organization. He assumes the major responsibility in this effort to build 'the ideal golf course.'

"'Bob' (as his intimates call him) regularly collaborated with me during the months of architectural designing. He rendered me assistance of incalculable value. I am convinced that from no one else could I have obtained such help. Bob is not only a student of golf, but of golf courses as well, and while I had known him for years, I was amazed at his knowledge and clear recollection of almost all of the particularly famous golf holes in England and Scotland, as well as America. Partly by reason of his taking a course in Engineering, during his college days, his suggestions were not only unique and original, but were practical.

"If, as I firmly believe, the Augusta National becomes the World's Wonder Inland Golf Course, this will be due to the original ideas that were contributed by Bob Jones.

"What is the 'ideal' course? Bob and I found ourselves in complete accord on these essentials:

1. A really great course must be pleasurable to the greatest possible number.
2. It must require strategy as well as skill, otherwise it cannot be enduringly interesting.
3. It must give the average player a fair chance and at the same time require the utmost from the expert who tries for sub-par scores.
4. All natural beauty should be preserved, natural hazards should be utilized, and a minimum of artificiality introduced.

"I want to say quite frankly that if our finished work is favorably received, it will be in part due to the excellent material at our disposal. We had plenty of land, towering pine forests, a large variety of other trees, beautiful shrubbery, streams of water, a mildly rolling terrain of great variety, a rich soil for growing good fairway grass and a naturally beautiful setting from an architectural standpoint.

"The property was originally settled by a Belgian Baron by the name of Berckmans. He was an ardent horticulturist and in this property he indulged in his hobby to the limit of his resources. I don't suppose the old Baron suspected that golf would some day become a popular sport in America and his property used by the World's greatest player for a golf course. But if Bob's great grandfather had foretold to the Baron what was to occur, the Baron could not possibly, in my opinion, have devised a beautification program that would today better serve our purposes.

"There are azaleas in abundance and a great variety of small plants, shrubbery and hedges, and a real cork tree. There are also scores of camellia bushes, that are now really trees—in size. But the most impressive of all is the ancient double row of Magnolia trees (said to be the finest in the South) that will border the driveway entrance to this 'Golfer's Paradise.'

"Now to get back to our golf course. Doubt may be expressed as to the possibility of making a course pleasurable to everyone, but it may be pointed out that the 'old Course' at St. Andrews, Scotland, which Bob likes best of all, very nearly approaches this ideal.

"It has been suggested that it was our intention at Augusta to produce copies of the most famous golf holes. Any attempt of this kind could only result in failure. It may be possible to reproduce a famous picture, but the charm of a golf hole may be dependent on a background of sand dunes, trees, or even mountains several miles away. A copy without the surroundings might create an unnatural appearance and cause a feeling of irritation, instead of charm. On the other hand, it is well to have a mental picture of the world's outstanding holes and to use this knowledge in reproducing their finest golfing features, and perhaps even improving on them.

"At Augusta we tried to produce eighteen ideal holes, not copies of classical holes but embodying their best features, with other features suggested by the nature of the terrain. We hope for accomplishments of such unique character that the holes will be looked upon as classics in themselves.

"The acid test of a golf course is its abiding popularity. And here we are up against a real difficulty. Does the average golfer know what he really likes himself? When he plays well he praises the course, but if his score is a high one the vigor of his language would put to shame a regimental sergeant major. It is usually the best holes that are condemned most vehemently by those who fail to solve their strategy. Bob Jones realizes this so strongly that when asked his opinion of the design of Augusta National he said the course would differ so markedly from others, that many of the members at first would have unpleasant things to say about the architects. A few years ago I would have agreed with Bob, but today, owing to his own teaching, the work and writings of C. B. MacDonald, Max Behr, Robert Hunter, and others, Americans appreciate real strategic golf to a greater extent than even in Scotland, Home of Golf.

"I do not believe the Augusta National will impress anyone as a long course, as although undulating it is not hilly. There are no irritating walks from greens to tees and moreover it will be so interesting and free from the annoyance of searching for lost balls, that players will get the impression that it is shorter than it really is."

Also included in the first Augusta National Invitation Tournament Program was an article on Fruitlands Nurseries' cofounder Prosper Julius Berckmans. Two of Prosper's three sons, Louis Alphonse Berckmans and Julius Alphonse Berckmans, followed in the family business in Augusta until their father's death in 1910. The brothers later played important roles in replanting and managing the Augusta National. The brothers co-wrote an article in the program that shed light on the old Fruitlands Nurseries and provided background information on their father, Prosper.

P. J. A. Berckmans

Prosper Julius Alphonse Berckmans, scholar, Horticulturalist, landscape architect, botanist and nurseryman, was born of Belgian nobility, at Arschot, Belgium, October 13, 1830. Died at Augusta, Georgia, November 8, 1910.

He attended school at Liere and Tourney, Belgium. In 1845, he went to France to the University of Tours where he graduated with honors in 1847. After this he studied botany in the Jardin des Plantes in Paris and the Botanical Gardens of Brussels.

Mr. Berckmans left Europe for religious and political reasons and came to the United States in 1850. He joined a party of sympathetic Belgians near Rome, Georgia. In 1851 his father Louis Edouard Mathieu Berckmans and his family came to New Jersey. There he joined them and purchased a large property and built a beautiful home in Plainfield, New Jersey.

In 1857 the Berckmans family moved to Augusta, Georgia where Mr. P. J. A. Berckmans established the nursery and in this nursery many valuable plants were originated and disseminated to different parts of the world. This great collection was tested as to its adaptability to the South, and those which did not measure up to the test went into the discard. In addition to the area in nurseries there were several acres under glass.

In 1898 the business was incorporated under the name of P. J. Berckmans Company, the incorporators being Prosper J. Berckmans, (and three sons) Louis A. Berckmans, Robert C. Berckmans, and P. J. A. Berckmans. In 1918 the charter expired and the P. J. Berckmans Company passed out of existence.

Mr. Berckmans originated, introduced and disseminated the following fruits and shrubs:

Originated

Peen-to Peach, Biota Aurea nana, Biota Auerea Conspicua, Biota Pyramidalis, Juniperus Communis Glauca, Elaneagnus Fruitlandi, Climbing Clothilde, Soupert Rose and several Althoeas.

Disseminated

Honey and Thurber Peaches, Bracket, Berenice, Picquet's Late, Oriole, Cora and Pallas Peaches, Texas Umbrella, Amur River Privet,

Double Yellow Jasmine, Citrus Trifoliata, Berckmans and Peter Wiley Grapes, several varieties of the best Azaleas and Camellias now in cultivation, several varieties of Japanese Persimmons, Coosa Nectarine, Stubb's Mulberry, Kelsey and Cumberland Plums, Mrs. Bryan, Hargrove, Haywood and Wallace Howard Apples.

In recognition of his work in horticulture he was honored by many societies in Europe and America. The University of Georgia conferred upon him the degree of Master of Science. He was likewise honored by the Society of Horticulture and Natural History of Montpelier, France, the Pomological Society of France, the Horticultural Society of Bordeaux and a number of others.

In 1876 he founded the Georgia State Horticultural Society, over which he presided until the date of his death. In 1887 he was elected President of the American Pomological Society. He resigned from the presidency in 1897.

In 1883–84 he went to Europe for the United States Government to collect horticultural exhibits for the New Orleans Exposition. In 1893 he presided over the Horticultural Congress in Chicago. [Berckmans was] Chairman of the Jury of Awards at the Jamestown Exposition in 1907, and was the only American to act as judge at the Centennial of the Royal Agriculture Society of Ghent in 1908.

In 1857 the Berckmans family moved to Augusta, Georgia where Mr. P. J. A. Berckmans established the nursery and in this nursery many valuable plants were originated and disseminated to different parts of the world.

March Madness The first Masters (Augusta National Invitation Tournament) was played March 22–25, 1934. The event is now contested each spring during the first full week in April. (Courtesy of Western Golf Association.)

Happy Horton
Bobby Jones congratulates Horton Smith on his winning the first Masters (Augusta National Invitation Tournament) in 1934. Horton became the tournament's first repeat winner when he won the event again in 1936. (Courtesy of Western Golf Association.)

Champions Gather Winners of the first six tournaments at Augusta National gather in 1940. Left to right: Horton Smith, 1934 and 1936; Byron Nelson, 1937; Gene Sarazen, 1935; Henry Picard, 1938; and Ralph Guldahl, 1939. (Courtesy of Western Golf Association.)

Invitation Exhibition Bobby Jones putts at the twelfth green during a well-attended exhibition match prior to the 1934 tournament. On the green (left to right) are Jones' playing partner and Augusta National head professional Ed Dudley, Dick Metz, Jones, and Ky Laffoon. (Photo by Tony Sheehan. Courtesy of Joseph M. Lee III.)

Practice Makes Perfect circa 2001 The Practice Green at the Augusta National Golf Club once served as the putting surface for a short 19th hole that Alister MacKenzie designed at Bobby Jones' request.

Olazábal Out, circa 1990 José Maria Olazábal, 1994 and 1999 champion, concentrates on getting safely out of one of the forty-five bunkers at the Augusta National Golf Club. (Courtesy of Joe Dromsky Collection.)

Casting Shadows

Ever notice that in most Masters Tournaments, the names at the top of the leaderboard look all too familiar? As a small group of repeat winners can attest, knowing the lay of Alister MacKenzie's masterpiece holds the key to the city. While Jack Nicklaus and Arnold Palmer own ten titles between them, a closer look at the numbers reveals a recurring theme throughout Masters history. More than sixty percent of tournaments played to date have been won by fifteen Masters multiple winners. Winning a green jacket in Augusta may be the hardest task facing a young golfer. But according to statistics, once a player has accomplished the feat, reigning as champion again in the future becomes a much easier quest.

Beginning with the first Augusta National Invitation Tournament in 1934, more than one of every three tournaments contested has been won by a member of the "Super Seven." Members of this elite group (Jack Nicklaus, Arnold Palmer, Jimmy Demaret, Sam Snead, Gary Player, Nick Faldo, and Tiger Woods) have each won the event at least three times. This exclusive group has captured 25 of the 68 Masters played to date.

Expand the inner circle to include the entire lot of fifteen players who have won on this Alister MacKenzie–designed golf course more than once and nearly two out of every three green jackets are accounted for. Even more impressive, this group of Masters multiple winners has captured 41 of the 68 Masters Tournaments played through 2004.

And it is not just the Masters champions who continue as models of consistency. There is also a pattern among those who have come close to winning the tournament—to continue to come close. Nine golfers who

Major Moment Jack Nicklaus, 1965 champion, is congratulated by co-second-place finishers Gary Player and Arnold Palmer and low amateur Downing Gray. Bobby Jones and Clifford Roberts are seated in front. (© Historic Golf Photos–Ron Watts Collection.)

have never won the Masters Tournament have multiple runner-up finishes, led by Tom Weiskopf with four and Greg Norman, Johnny Miller, and Tom Kite with three each. Harry Cooper, Lloyd Mangrum, Ken Venturi, David Duval, and Davis Love III round out a list of Masters non-winners who have each finished second in the tournament on two occasions.

In 68 Masters Tournaments played to date, thirty-four participants have multiple first- or second-place finishes. Since the tournament began, twenty-two golfers have managed to finish second on more than

Settle Down Ben Crenshaw beckons to his golf ball following a third-round tee shot in the 1989 Masters. Crenshaw finished in a tie with Greg Norman just one shot in back of Scott Hoch and eventual champion Nick Faldo. (Courtesy of Joe Dromsky Collection.)

one occasion. Aside from Weiskopf, former Masters champions Jack Nicklaus and Ben Hogan have each finished runner-up four times. While Miller, Norman, and Kite have each been the bridesmaid on three occasions, champions Tom Watson and Raymond Floyd also have three Masters second-place finishes.

Mirroring the status quo since the start of the Masters Tournament in 1934, the storyline over the past quarter-century shows much the same trend: win

once in Augusta and the odds of winning again are greatly tilted in a golfer's favor. Since 1980 alone, Seve Ballesteros has won the tournament twice (1980 and '83), and Ben Crenshaw has lined his locker with green jackets won eleven years apart (1984 and '95). Bernhard Langer has also won twice over two decades (in 1985 and '93); José Maria Olazábal has captured his pair of wins (in 1994 and '99); and Nick Faldo (in 1989, '90, and '96) and Tiger Woods (in 1997, '01, and

'02) have each won three times during that span. Throw in
Tom Watson's second Masters title in 1981 and Jack Nicklaus' record sixth win in 1986 for good measure and the picture of dominance by multiple winners becomes even more clear.

Sixteen of the last 25 tournaments (64 percent) have gone to golfers who have won the event more than once. With recent non-multiple Masters champions Vijay Singh, Mike Weir, and Phil Mickelson all in their primes, there is a good chance they too might impact the winners circle again. Three-time champion Tiger Woods could also be a force for years to come.

The following list highlights the repeat winners in the Masters Tournament since 1980.

1980—Seve Ballesteros
1981—Tom Watson
1982—Craig Stadler
1983—Seve Ballesteros
1984—Ben Crenshaw
1985—Bernhard Langer
1986—Jack Nicklaus
1987—Larry Mize
1988—Sandy Lyle
1989—Nick Faldo
1990—Nick Faldo
1991—Ian Woosnam
1992—Fred Couples
1993—Bernhard Langer
1994—José Maria Olazábal
1995—Ben Crenshaw
1996—Nick Faldo
1997—Tiger Woods
1998—Mark O'Meara
1999—José Maria Olazábal
2000—Vijay Singh
2001—Tiger Woods
2002—Tiger Woods
2003—Mike Weir

Nicklaus and Norman circa 2002 In addition to the six green jackets won by Jack Nicklaus, he and Greg Norman have combined to finish runner-up in the Masters Tournament on seven occasions.

Of the Masters' multiple champions, it took Ben Crenshaw the longest—thirteen tries—to win his first Masters, then another eleven years to win again. Another Ben, Hogan, waited ten years before claiming his first Masters Tournament, then won two times in three years. In the span of eleven tournaments between 1942 and 1955, Hogan finished second twice before winning two times, then finished runner-up twice more. Craig Wood and Ralph Guldahl also each finished second twice before winning the Masters Tournament.

In the five Masters Tournaments contested between 1951 and 1955, Hogan either won or finished runner-up. Hogan is also the only participant in Masters history to lose in a playoff twice, both of

On eight occasions in Masters history a participant has followed a second-place finish with a victory the next year.

which were of the eighteen-hole variety. Nick Faldo is the only golfer to win twice in playoffs, both in sudden death, in back-to-back years nonetheless, and both at the eleventh hole.

Nine multiple Masters winners (Nicklaus 6, Palmer 4, Player 3, Snead 3, Crenshaw 2, Ballesteros 2, Watson 2, Hogan 2, and Nelson 2) have also placed second on more than one occasion (see listing, page 133). Two-time champion José Maria Olazábal has also tasted the bitter fruits of a second-place finish, but on only one occasion. The five remaining multiple Masters winners pride themselves on winning when they've gotten close and have never finished second (Tiger Woods 3, Nick Faldo 3, Jimmy Demaret 3, Bernhard Langer 2, and Horton Smith 2). Four champions with one green jacket (Raymond Floyd, Ralph Guldahl, Carry Middlecoff, and Craig Wood) have each finished in the runner-up spot more than once.

From 1956 through 1965, the Masters was dominated by Jack Nicklaus, Arnold Palmer, and Gary Player, who combined for victories in eight of nine years, including seven straight. Gary Player managed the first of three green jackets during the 1961 Masters, when Palmer finished in a tie for second. The following year, Palmer and Player traded places. When Palmer won again in 1964, Jack Nicklaus finished runner-up. The next year, 1965, Nicklaus reversed the situation, leaving Palmer and Player tied for the runner-up spot.

Just as puzzling are the next seven tournaments between 1967 and 1973 when only Nicklaus (1972)

won again. In addition, those seven events saw six first-time champions (Gay Brewer, 1967; Bob Goalby, 1968; George Archer, 1969; Billy Casper, 1970; Charles Coody, 1971; and Tommy Aaron, 1973) that would not win another tournament. This marks the longest streak of non-multiple winners in Masters history, though to their credit, Brewer and Casper each finished second the year before winning.

On eight occasions in Masters history a participant has followed a second-place finish with a victory the next year. Jack Nicklaus has accomplished the feat twice, and Ralph Guldahl, Byron Nelson, Arnold Palmer, Gay Brewer, Billy Casper, and Ben Crenshaw once each. And while it is likely that there is a better than average chance of winning again in Augusta, chances are not good that the feat will be accomplished in back-to-back years. Of the fifteen multiple Masters winners just three have won the Masters in consecutive years: Jack Nicklaus in 1965 and '66, Nick Faldo in 1989 and '90, and Tiger Woods in 2001 and '02.

Of the first 18 Masters Tournaments staged from 1934 through 1954 (minus three years off for World War II), a dozen green jackets were divided among just five golfers: Horton Smith (1934 and '36), Byron Nelson (1937 and '42), Jimmy Demaret (1940, '47 and '50), Ben Hogan (1951 and '53), and Sam Snead (1949, '52 and '54).

The cause and effect of these statistics is due in no small part to four underlying yet overwhelming factors. The first is the course factor. The Augusta National

Faldo's Fortune
Nick Faldo watches his putt in the final round of the 1990 tournament that he won in a playoff for the second consecutive year. (Courtesy of Joe Dromsky Collection.)

Lean Too Team Ballesteros attempts to coax in a putt during the 1988 tournament in which the two-time winner (1980 and 1983) finished in a tie for eleventh place. (Courtesy of Joe Dromsky Collection.)

is the only major staged over the same tract of land annually. Conventional wisdom holds that the more times a golfer competes over a particular design, the more local knowledge gained, the better the odds of winning.

Once a player has finally figured out MacKenzie's puzzle and has won the Masters Tournament, the experience factor kicks in. That is when the invitations keep coming for an entire lifetime, and the local knowledge begins to play an even bigger factor. Age, it seems, is not so much a factor at the Augusta National and, within reason, can actually work in a golfer's favor. Take Jack Nicklaus for example, of how far experience (coupled with sheer determination and mental toughness) can carry a golfer over MacKenzie's layout. Winning six green jackets over the span of twenty-four years, Master Jack saved one his best performances for the 1998 Masters. At age fifty-eight, some thirty-six years removed from his first Masters title, Nicklaus defied all odds and contended again, this time while nursing a bad hip. With a birdie at number seven on Masters Sunday, Nicklaus pulled into a tie for second before eventually finishing in a tie for sixth place. While nobody compares to Nicklaus in this regard, Gary Player posted three wins in Augusta over eighteen years. Raymond Floyd's win in 1976 and second-place finish in 1992 at age forty-nine is another good example of the experience factor at work in Augusta.

That is where the field factor enters in. With the smallest field of any major, and even smaller when you omit the golfers who do not have a snowball's chance in Augusta of winning, it is not hard to see that once a golfer has won over MacKenzie's design, he keeps coming back to contend again. Another advantage in favor of former champions is their ability to deal with the always present pressure factor in Augusta.

In the course of Masters Tournament history there have been 68 champion and 96 runner-up spots (due to ties) awarded. One hundred thirteen of the 164 available first- and second-place slots (69 percent) have been claimed by the following group of just 34 golfers.

This group of multiple winners and runners-up has proven its dominance of MacKenzie's design and repeatedly has been a force in Masters history.

	Wins	Second
Jack Nicklaus	6	4
Arnold Palmer	4	2
Gary Player	3	2
Tiger Woods	3	–
Jimmy Demaret	3	–
Sam Snead	3	2
Nick Faldo	3	–
Horton Smith	2	–
Byron Nelson	2	2
Ben Hogan	2	4
Tom Watson	2	3
Seve Ballesteros	2	2
Bernhard Langer	2	–
Ben Crenshaw	2	2
José Maria Olazábal	2	1
Raymond Floyd	1	3
Ralph Guldahl	1	2
Cary Middlecoff	1	2
Craig Wood	1	2
Gay Brewer Jr.	1	1
Billy Casper	1	1
Doug Ford	1	1
Jack Burke Jr.	1	1
Fred Couples	1	1
Tom Weiskopf	–	4
Johnny Miller	–	3
Greg Norman	–	3
Tom Kite	–	3
Harry Cooper	–	2
Lloyd Mangrum	–	2
Ken Venturi	–	2
David Duval	–	2
Davis Love III	–	2
Ernie Els	–	2

Watson's First Tom Watson receives a famed green jacket from Raymond Floyd following his Masters win in 1977. He would repeat the feat in 1981. (© Historic Golf Photos – Ron Watts Collection)

Almost as mystifying is the Masters career of Fuzzy Zoeller, who proves to be an anomaly on two counts. First, to his credit, Zoeller's win in 1979 distinguishes him as the lone participant since Gene Sarazen in 1935 to win on his first trip to Augusta. The feat gains even more credence when one considers that the entire field was new to the course in 1935. A quick glance at tournament history reinforces the natural conclusion that Zoeller would have better than fair odds of returning to the green jacket ceremony, or at the very least contending for another title. But since winning the Masters on his first try at age twenty-seven, Zoeller again proves the exception, placing no better than a tie for tenth in 1982.

Once dominated by golfers from the United States, the statistic no longer holds true for the Masters Tournament. Since Gary Player (the tournament's first international champion) won his second Masters title in 1974, green jackets have been nearly equally distributed to golfers who were born outside the country, with U.S. golfers holding a scant sixteen-to-fifteen edge. Even more telling are the numbers since Sandy Lyle's victory in 1988. Ten of seventeen Masters Champions since that time have been members of the international contingent.

The bottom line? If history repeats itself as it has over the past eight decades of Masters Tournament history, it is just a matter of time before Tiger Woods and a handful of other former champions don yet another green jacket; half of those will be from the international field. It's all in the numbers.

Team Tiger circa 2001 Tiger Woods on the practice green with caddy Steve Williams during Masters Week 2001 when he won his second green jacket. Woods' caddy during his first win in 1997, Mike "Fluff" Cowan (far right) looks on.

Masters Tournament Results
Listed in bold are the 34 golfers who have either won the Masters and/or finished in second place more than once.

Year	Winner	2nd Place	Year	Winner	2nd Place
2004	Phil Mickelson	**Ernie Els**	1979	Fuzzy Zoeller	Ed Sneed, **Tom Watson** (sudden death playoff)
2003	Mike Weir	Len Mattiace (sudden death playoff)	1978	**Gary Player**	Rod Funseth, Hubert Green, **Tom Watson**
2002	**Tiger Woods**	Retief Goosen	1977	**Tom Watson**	**Jack Nicklaus**
2001	**Tiger Woods**	**David Duval**	1976	**Raymond Floyd**	**Ben Crenshaw**
2000	Vijay Singh	**Ernie Els**	1975	**Jack Nicklaus**	**Johnny Miller**, **Tom Weiskopf**
1999	**José Maria Olazábal**	Davis Love III			
1998	Mark O'Meara	**Fred Couples**, **David Duval**	1974	**Gary Player**	Dave Stockton, **Tom Weiskopf**
1997	**Tiger Woods**	**Tom Kite**	1973	Tommy Aaron	J. C. Snead
1996	**Nick Faldo**	**Greg Norman**	1972	**Jack Nicklaus**	Bruce Crampton, Bobby Mitchell, **Tom Weiskopf**
1995	**Ben Crenshaw**	Davis Love III			
1994	**José Maria Olazábal**	Tom Lehman	1971	Charles Coody	**Johnny Miller**, **Jack Nicklaus**
1993	**Bernhard Langer**	Chip Beck			
1992	**Fred Couples**	**Raymond Floyd**	1970	**Billy Casper**	Gene Littler (18-hole playoff)
1991	Ian Woosnam	**José Maria Olazábal**			
1990	**Nick Faldo**	**Raymond Floyd** (sudden death playoff)	1969	George Archer	**Billy Casper**, George Knudson, **Tom Weiskopf**
1989	**Nick Faldo**	Scott Hoch (sudden death playoff)	1968	Bob Goalby	Roberto De Vicenzo
1988	Sandy Lyle	Mark Calcavecchia	1967	**Gay Brewer Jr.**	Bobby Nichols
1987	Larry Mize	**Greg Norman**, **Seve Ballesteros** (sudden death playoff)	1966	**Jack Nicklaus**	Tommy Jacobs, **Gay Brewer Jr.** (18-hole playoff)
1986	**Jack Nicklaus**	**Tom Kite**, **Greg Norman**	1965	**Jack Nicklaus**	**Arnold Palmer**, **Gary Player**
1985	**Bernhard Langer**	**Seve Ballesteros**, **Raymond Floyd**	1964	**Arnold Palmer**	Dave Marr, **Jack Nicklaus**
1984	**Ben Crenshaw**	**Tom Watson**			
1983	**Seve Ballesteros**	**Ben Crenshaw**, **Tom Kite**	1963	**Jack Nicklaus**	Tony Lema
1982	Craig Stadler	Dan Pohl (sudden death playoff)	1962	**Arnold Palmer**	**Gary Player**, Dow Finsterwald (18-hole playoff)
1981	**Tom Watson**	**Johnny Miller**, **Jack Nicklaus**	1961	**Gary Player**	Charles Coe, **Arnold Palmer**
1980	**Seve Ballesteros**	Gibby Gilbert, Jack Newton	1960	**Arnold Palmer**	Ken Venturi

Year	Winner	2nd Place
1959	Art Wall Jr.	Cary Middlecoff
1958	Arnold Palmer	Doug Ford, Fred Hawkins
1957	Doug Ford	Sam Snead
1956	Jack Burke Jr.	Ken Venturi
1955	Cary Middlecoff	Ben Hogan
1954	Sam Snead	Ben Hogan (18-hole playoff)
1953	Ben Hogan	Ed Oliver Jr.
1952	Sam Snead	Jack Burke Jr.
1951	Ben Hogan	Skee Riegel
1950	Jimmy Demaret	Jim Ferrier
1949	Sam Snead	Johnny Bulla, Lloyd Mangrum
1948	Claude Harmon	Cary Middlecoff
1947	Jimmy Demaret	Byron Nelson, Frank Stranahan
1946	Herman Keiser	Ben Hogan
1945	Cancelled during World War II	
1944	Cancelled during World War II	
1943	Cancelled during World War II	
1942	Byron Nelson	Ben Hogan (18-hole playoff)
1941	Craig Wood	Byron Nelson
1940	Jimmy Demaret	Lloyd Mangrum
1939	Ralph Guldahl	Sam Snead
1938	Henry Picard	Harry Cooper, Ralph Guldahl
1937	Byron Nelson	Ralph Guldahl
1936	Horton Smith	Harry Cooper
1935	Gene Sarazen	Craig Wood (18-hole playoff)
1934	Horton Smith	Craig Wood

Like Father, Like Son Jack and Jackie Nicklaus react to the pressures of Masters Tournament play. Nicklaus placed among the top five finishers in the event eighteen times. (Courtesy Joe Dromsky Collection)

Technology's Impact
As he looked over his "Calamity Jane" putter with Tony Manero, Bobby Jones could scarcely have envisioned how the course he created would weather the test of time through the technological changes to come to the game of golf. (© Historic Golf Photos - Ron Watts Collection.)

Men of Vision

Since the start of the Industrial Revolution, technology has impacted the world in a major way, the world of sports included. These incremental changes over time were of paramount concern to Alister MacKenzie, who poured a maximum of mental labor into designs he suspected might one day become obsolete. MacKenzie's design talent lay in his grasp of hairline differences between subtleties and nuances and his feel for incorporating them naturally into the landscapes on his canvas. Bobby Jones painted with far bolder strokes and was destined to drastically alter the boundaries set before him. MacKenzie was a graduate of Cambridge, with a mind for science, and Jones the engineer from Georgia Tech. MacKenzie had long been a proponent of limited-flight golf balls, while Jones was a driving force in technology's transition from hickory-shafted clubs to steel. At sixty-two, MacKenzie was Old School, and Jones, thirty, represented the new age. That these two visionaries worked together to design Jones' dream speaks volumes to their commitment to the integrity of the game and likely holds the key to the Augusta National's longstanding success.

Prior to 1930, golf's ruling body overseas, the Royal and Ancient Golf Club in Scotland, refused to approve the use of steel-shafted golf clubs. It was not until after Great Britain had defeated the United States 7-5 in the 1929 Ryder Cup Matches played out over MacKenzie's hometown course at Moortown that the Royal and Ancient reversed its stance. The loss hardly came as a surprise as the entire American team faced what proved an insurmountable handicap during the competition, not as much from the opposition as their reliance on technology. The USGA announced the approval of steel-shafted clubs in 1924 and the American team that featured Walter Hagen, Gene Sarazen, and Johnny Farrell had long made the switch to steel-shafted clubs. At Moortown, American team was forced to find suitable hickory-shafted clubs. A young member on the American team, Horton Smith was forced to play clubs of the hickory-shafted variety for the first time during the matches. Incidentally, Smith won his singles match for the United States. But the future was steel and the clubs gained even more appeal when Jones struck an endorsement deal to promote them with the A.G. Spalding Company beginning in 1932.

While MacKenzie and Jones could not possibly know the full extent of technology's impact on the game, these two visionaries had a notion of where the game was headed. While they did not have a crystal ball into the future, they did have MacKenzie's long-established thirteen rules of golf architecture to guide them. When the duo laid out the design for the Augusta National Golf Club in the summer of 1932, MacKenzie's timeless rules became their checks and balances. These provisions ensured that Jones' dream course would be "elastic" to accommodate future lengthening. Another of MacKenzie's rules stipulated that no two consecutive holes be set in the same direction. Incorporating these simple design laws into the overall plan made certain the layout would accept major alterations over time without disruption to the previous hole. MacKenzie and Jones also designed the Augusta National to play to 6,700 yards, longer than other championship courses in the United States with the exception of Oakmont.

Before the 1930s came to a close, Jones might have

MacKenzie reasoned that "One got just as much fun in driving the old 'Haskell' ball twenty yards farther than one's opponent as today one gets in hitting the small heavy ball twenty yards farther."

wondered aloud if his dream golf course had already been rendered obsolete by the standards he and MacKenzie originally put in play. During the first round of the 1935 Masters an unheard of ten golfers broke par, leading the *Augusta Chronicle* to follow with the heading, "O.B. Keeler Is Perturbed as Big Berthas Bombard Augusta National Course." "Old Man Par" was still a much revered score in the 1930s and according to Keeler, "here, at the end of Round 1, is the Old Man back in his corner, bleeding from both gills...." Byron Nelson's opening-round 66 in the 1937 Masters served further notice of the power of steel and the wave of technology to come. It was Jones himself who helped popularize the inevitable. The once-in-a-lifetime wooden-shafted legend endorsed mass-produced steel-shafted Bobby Jones model golf clubs by A.G. Spalding and Brothers. The clubs remained a big seller for the better part of the next half-century. While Jones' steel-shafted clubs changed the way the game was played, it was science's effect on golf balls that concerned MacKenzie even more.

As far back as the early 1930s when he penned his second book, *The Spirit of St. Andrews*, the visionary in MacKenzie recognized that golf balls would continually be altered by science to attain greater distance. Concerned that the flight of golf balls was out of hand and that golf courses had grown too long, he noted that already "there is too much walking and too little golf," and felt the need for limited-flight golf balls. In his candid opinion, golf's ruling bodies should have taken drastic action on the subject many years earlier. "The Royal and Ancient 'rules of golf' committee intimate that they will put a stop to any new ball which flies appreciably further, but the difficulty is how can they? There may not be any sudden change which would warrant them intervening. On the other hand I feel sure that during the last few years improvements have been made in the manufacture of golf balls which enable them to fly two or three yards further every year...." What was painfully evident to MacKenzie nearly a century ago has come to pass. "There is little the golf architect can do to remedy this," MacKenzie maintained, "except to point out from his experience and knowledge of psychology what is likely to give the greatest enjoyment to the greatest number."

MacKenzie reasoned that "One got just as much fun in driving the old 'Haskell' ball twenty yards farther than one's opponent as today one gets in hitting the small heavy ball twenty yards farther." Drawing a comparison to other sports, MacKenzie wrote that "Quite as big a thrill is obtained in hitting a baseball or cricket ball a hundred yards as a golf ball two hundred." If the distance attained by golf balls was cause for concern in the early part of the 1900s, how much more impassioned MacKenzie would be on the subject today. There was even talk in some circles of penalizing golfers for hitting the golf ball too far.

While MacKenzie was in favor of a limited-flight golf ball, he also realized that distance needed to be rewarded since it was "more frequently achieved by skill and grace than by mere brute force." Similarly, an accurate golfer with less distance was to be rewarded over an opponent able to hit the ball farther, but erratically.

At the heart of MacKenzie's concern regarding distance was the feeling that golfers were "losing the joy of playing the variety of approach shots that were so necessary in the old days." In essence, the new technology rendered obsolete the strategy he toiled to inject into his designs. The tactician in MacKenzie likened golf to the thinking man's game of chess, in which each move was strategic in the overall picture. In MacKenzie's view, playing every second shot as a pitch into the green rendered the game a bore.

Moreover, MacKenzie correctly reasoned that the distance of a golf ball's flight was relative and the temporary gain a golfer attained from the affect of science would soon be neutralized by an opponent using the same equipment. He even suggested moving the tees up a bit to accommodate a limited-flight ball, giving golfers the effect that they were hitting as far, just another example of the master illusionist in MacKenzie at work. The use of limited-flight golf balls, MacKenzie reasoned, would result in a game with less walking, more golf, and take considerably less time to play. The

famed architect noted that "twenty years ago we played three rounds of golf in a day and considered we had taken an interminably long time if we took more than two hours to play a round."

By 1931, the USGA adopted a "balloon ball" no smaller than 1.68 inches and no heavier than 1.5 ounces. MacKenzie speculated that this might pave the way for the introduction of what he referred to as "a floater," an even larger ball. "A floater will be a much more pleasurable ball to play with," wrote MacKenzie, "but it is possible and even probable that even this may not solve our problem of restricting the flight of the ball."

Taking into account the array of technological advancements over the past century, if Jones and MacKenzie designed the Augusta National today, there is little doubt their layout would be quite different. But of this there should be no question: the soul of the Augusta National would be strikingly similar, a showcase of wide-open play and mighty undulations, of large, fast putting surfaces with subtle and unnerving nuances. It would remain a challenge to golf's mighty and prove uplifting to those of lesser skill. To MacKenzie's credit, the failsafe design sculpted naturally over 365 acres of the old Berckmans Plantation was built to accommodate change gracefully. In the wake of technological advances from Jones-endorsed Spalding steel-shafted golf clubs to Tiger Woods' Nike One golf balls, the Augusta National has also evolved. Indeed, a century from now this finest design in golf will be altered in ways we cannot envision. But with the compass put in place by MacKenzie and Jones long ago providing direction for future change and a constant reminder of their lasting imprint, the grand golf course they created will continue to weather the test of time admirably.

The Back Nine

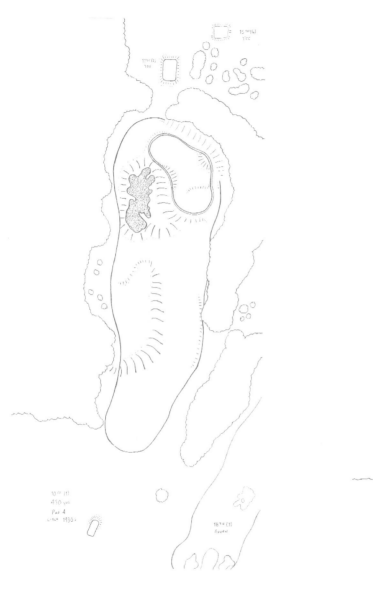

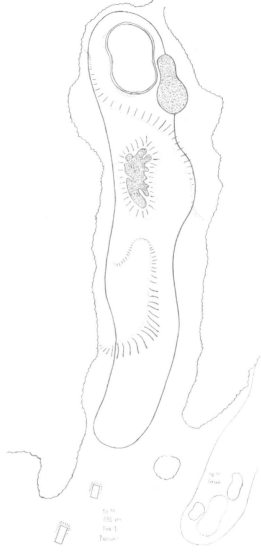

CIRCA 1930s

PRESENT

HOLE 10
Reversal of Fortunes

MAJOR CHANGES

1937
Putting surface moved back and elevated away from large "MacKenzie Bunker" in fairway.

1937
Right greenside bunker added.

1968
Right greenside bunker enlarged and pothole bunker removed.

1972
Tee box relocated 10 yards to the left.

2002
Tee box moved back 5–10 yards and left 5 yards.

Hole 10, circa 1934 The original tenth green is shown here next to the largest bunker on the course, which has come to be known as the MacKenzie Bunker. When the first Augusta National Invitation Tournament took place in 1934, the nines were reversed and this served as the opening hole. Due to drainage concerns it was also the first hole to undergo a major alteration. In 1937 an elevated green was built in back of the original putting surface by Perry Maxwell. (Photo by Tony Sheehan. Courtesy of Joseph M. Lee III.)

par	4	
1934 yardage	430	CAMELLIA
1959 yardage	470	
current yardage	495	
difficulty	1	

"This is a comparatively easy down-hill hole. A long drive over hillocks on the right will land on a plateau from which an iron shot can be played to the opening of a large nature-made punch bowl green. The driver that pulls his shot to the left of the fairway is called upon to play a difficult second shot over a large spectacular bunker, with small chance of getting near the pin. This hole embodies the most attractive features of the Thirteenth Hole at Cypress Point, California, and the Fourth at Alwoodley, one of the best of the British inland links."

—ALISTER MACKENZIE, 1932

Hole History

At approximately 10 A.M. on the morning of March 22, 1934, Ralph Stonehouse hit the first shot in Masters Tournament history down the current tenth fairway. The 1934 tournament, won by Horton Smith, was the only event in which the course played in reverse order. The current front nine received more sunlight and less frost than the back side. To alleviate potential delays in start times, Jones had the nines reverted to the order he and MacKenzie originally envisioned. Two years later Smith won the Masters for a second time with the layout in the new but even older order.

One of the longest par 4s in major golf history, this sweeping downhill dogleg-left drops off more than 100 feet in elevation from tee to green. While MacKenzie noted it as a "comparatively easy down-hill hole," the tenth at Augusta National has been lengthened by 65 yards. The tenth hole ranks as the hardest hole of the tournament and marks the first of three consecutive holes among the top-five toughest all-time at the Augusta National. The program for the first Augusta National Invitation Tournament in 1934 features the golf course in reverse order from the layout played today. Although the tenth hole has traditionally played the hardest, it was ranked eighth in the 2004 Masters.

MacKenzie originally designed this downhill dogleg left to play 65 yards shorter and with today's large fairway bunker to the left of the green. Due to drainage problems at the bottom of a nearly 100-foot drop in elevation, the putting surface was redesigned in 1937. MacKenzie associate Perry Maxwell rebuilt a new putting surface 150 feet farther back on higher ground. The

MacKenzie originally designed this downhill dogleg left to play 65 yards shorter and with today's large fairway bunker to the left of the green.

"MacKenzie bunker" in the middle of the tenth fairway occupies 5,862 square feet and is likely the lone bunker from the original design that still remains. It measures 59 yards, 24 yards longer than the depth of the tenth putting surface. This marked the first of two major changes to the course that year, both performed by Maxwell, who then turned his thoughts to reconstructing a new seventh green protected by bunkers.

By the time MacKenzie penned his second book in the early 1930s (and published for the first time in 1995), his *Spirit of St. Andrews* offering included a change of mind regarding course drainage. While earlier in his career he felt he knew more about the subject than most, "Today I realize that drainage is a specialist engineer's job and that a club gets far better results and less costly work in employing a man who has devoted his whole time to it." From the tenth tee to the eleventh green the elevation change at the Augusta National is over 150 feet downhill.

Memorable Moments

Only four golfers have played this hole at 3-under par during an entire tournament: Jerry Heard (1974), Jack Newton (1979), Nick Price (1991), and Jim Furyk (1998).

"There is a large spectacular bunker (MacKenzie bunker) guarding the green on the left which makes a difficult second shot for the player who has placed his drive on the left side of the fairway. The player who has taken the correct line over a succession of hillocks on the right-hand side is presented with an easy second shot into an opening that leads to a nature-made punch bowl green."

—*NEW YORK TIMES, 1933*

Tenth Tee, circa 1948 Early view of the tenth hole at the Augusta National Golf Club as viewed from the tee.
(© Historic Golf Photos– Ron Watts Collection.)

"The tee is on high ground and, I might add, immediately in front of my cabin. The fairway goes down a broad slope from the tee, following on the left a straight line to the green, but on the right, fanning out to a considerable width. Since the hole is of good length for a par 4, it is decidedly advantageous for the player to make use of the run offered by this slope. Therefore, the line of play is down the left side as closely as one may dare. A tee shot played to the right which does not avail itself of the slope will add at least two club numbers to the length of the second shot."

—BOBBY JONES, 1959

Highs and Lows

Two tournaments have ended in sudden death at the tenth hole. In 1982 Craig Stadler won the green jacket when Dan Pohl bogeyed this first playoff hole.

In 2003 Mike Weir defeated Len Mattiace in the sixth sudden death in Masters history and twelfth play-off overall. Mattiace had fashioned a brilliant closing round of 65, but his only bogey at the seventy-second hole proved a harbinger. When Mattiace could manage no better than double-bogey on the first playoff hole, Mike Weir sank his bogey putt for the victory.

Six golfers have scored an eagle on this hole and six others have doubled par at the tenth during Masters competition. Master participants who have provided eagle heroics are Dick Metz (1940), Doug Ford (1960), Rick Fehr (1987), Guy Yamamoto (1995), Jumbo Ozaki (1999), and Casey Wittenberg (2004).

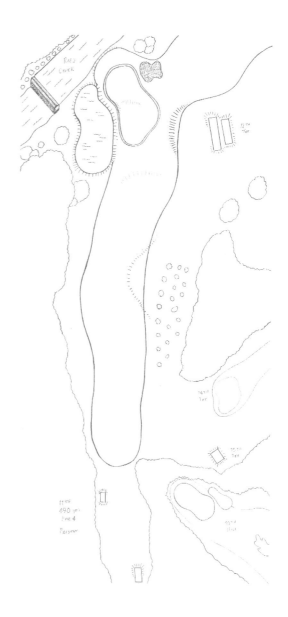

CIRCA 1930s

PRESENT

HOLE 11
Playoff Pride

Hole 11, circa 1934 The original eleventh hole designed by Alister MacKenzie played from in back of the tenth hole and featured a tributary from Rae's Creek running along the left side of the green. In 1950, a new fairway was cut through the trees behind the tenth green and the greenside tributary was made into a pond. (Photo by Tony Sheehan. Courtesy of Joseph M. Lee III.)

MAJOR CHANGES

1950
Hole redesigned to include pond, new tee box and fairway opening, and reshaped putting surface.

1953
Pair of back greenside bunkers added.

1990
Green rebuilt (following flood damage along Rae's Creek)

1999
Alterations to putting surface, greenside bunker, and pond.

2002
Tee box relocated 30–35 yards back and right.

2002
Section of landing area regraded.

		WHITE DOGWOOD
par	4	
1934 yardage	415	
1959 yardage	445	
current yardage	490	
difficulty	4	

Eleventh Green, circa 1950s The eleventh green as it appeared shortly after the addition of the greenside pond. Note the small footbridge to the left of the water. (Courtesy of Summerville Photo.)

Hole History

Designed by Alister MacKenzie to play 415 yards, this hole has undergone the largest alteration in length made to any one hole since the first Masters Tournament. It now plays 75 yards longer than originally built. A pond is situated to the left of the green, with a greenside bunker protecting the back-right of the putting surface. The start of "Amen Corner", this is the first of five holes at which water comes into play on the back nine. Through the 1950 tournament, Rae's Creek

also ran along the left side and extended to the left front of the eleventh green. After the tournament ended, the hole underwent a major overhaul and was redesigned with a new tee box to the far left side of the tenth green and included a new fairway cut through the trees. Rae's Creek was dammed to create the pond that now guards the left side of the current green. Back then, a small footbridge to the left side of the pond gave golfers an alternate route to the back of the green. The new changes not only lengthened the hole but brought

"The green is situated in the bend of a stream. The approach has a marked tilt upwards from left to right, so that the further and more accurately a drive is placed to the left the easier the second shot becomes. This should always be a most fascinating hole. I don't know another quite like it."

—ALISTER MACKENZIE, 1932

water more into play. When Ben Hogan surveyed the changes prior to the 1951 Masters, he decided the risk-reward of going for the green on the approach was far too great and promptly declared, "If you ever see me on the eleventh green in two, you'll know I missed my second shot."

Raymond Floyd would have done well to heed Hogan's advice forty tournaments later. It was the eleventh where Floyd's hopes of a Masters title at age forty-seven were dashed when his ball found the water on the second playoff hole against Nick Faldo in 1990. The winner of that year's Par-3 Contest, Floyd also came closest to breaking the so-called jinx that no winner of the Wednesday tournament has ever advanced to win the main event in the same year. Major changes also impacted the hole prior to the 2002 tournament when the tee was moved back 35 yards and against the right-side tree line.

While Faldo celebrated back-to-back green jackets at the hole, the green was washed away in major flooding along Rae's Creek in the fall of 1990. During the span of a day-and-a-half, twelve and a half inches of rain fell on the city of Augusta. Water overflowed from swollen banks throughout Augusta, washing out roads and the eleventh green and its surroundings. By late November the putting surface, as well as the pond and dam to its left side, was temporarily rebuilt

to its previous dimensions. Following the 1991 Masters Tournament, the area was rebuilt again, this time permanently.

Memorable Moments

The eleventh has proven the deciding hole in four of six Masters sudden death playoffs. In 1979, Fuzzy Zoeller made birdie at the eleventh in the first sudden death in Masters history to defeat Ed Sneed and Tom Watson. Native Augustan Larry Mize sank a historic 140-foot pitch shot in the 1987 playoff to defeat Greg Norman, with Seve Ballesteros eliminated at the tenth hole. Mize's shot against the heavily favored Norman produced a David-versus-Goliath finish that stunned the golf world and engrained in golf consciousness the vision of Mize leaping to great heights on the hole. With both golfers lying two and Norman already on the putting surface, Norman the Australian is reported to have turned to his caddie and prophetically whispered that Mize couldn't get down in two from where his ball was located (to the right side of the sloped putting surface). Later, Norman confided to the media that his opinion had been right.

After winning, Larry Mize shared his joy: "That ball, I waited for it to go in, I wasn't going to jump before it went in, and I just went in orbit. You know, I told 'em I could probably, I can't dunk it [a basketball], but I

Déjà Vu, 1990 Nick Faldo reacts after winning in a playoff for the second straight year at the eleventh hole. Four shots down with six holes to play, Faldo charged back with three back-nine birdies to tie Raymond Floyd in regulation. (Courtesy of Joe Dromsky Collection.)

probably could have then. But it was just great and as I said earlier the fans were great and I was just very fortunate to be able to, be able to win this."

Nick Faldo won back-to-back Masters Tournaments at the hole in playoffs in 1989 (versus Scott Hoch) and in 1990 (against Raymond Floyd). "I would really like to be able to build that one [eleventh hole] at home. I'll have to buy some more land and re-create that one, because that's, you know, something special. Obviously I can't believe… I mean what's the odds on one guy winning two years on a shot at the same hole is unbelievable." In doing so Faldo joined Jack Nicklaus (1965 and 1966) and, later, Tiger Woods (2001 and 2002) as the only golfers to win the tournament in consecutive years.

Highs and Lows

Seven golfers have played the par-4 eleventh hole at 3-under par during a Masters Tournament, the most notable being Curtis Strange in 1985. One of the few bright spots in Strange's opening-round 80 was a birdie at the hole, which he also birdied the next two days. He could have used another birdie on Sunday, the only day he did not post a three on the hole, as his bid for a green jacket fell one shot shy at the end of regulation play.

The hole has yielded just three eagles in Masters Tournament history, all after Hogan's refrain in 1951 that he would never again risk playing his second shot to the newly designed and well-protected green. Jerry Barber (1962), Brad Faxon (2002), and K. J. Choi (2004) are the only golfers to have scored an eagle at the eleventh hole.

Three others have posted record nines at the par-4 hole: Dow Finsterwald (1952), Bo Wininger (1958), and William G. Moody III (1980).

"The tee shot to this hole is blind in that the fairway upon which the ball is to land is not visible from the tee. Nevertheless, the limits of the fairway are sufficiently well-defined by the trees on either side. A drive down the left side of the fairway provides better visibility of the forward portions of the green, but slightly to the right of center is better should the pin be located on the promontory of the green extending into the water hazard on the left. The second shot is usually played with a 3-iron or a stronger club, and a player must be bold and confident indeed to go for the pin when it is in this location."

—BOBBY JONES, 1959

Eleventh Tee, circa 1994 The tee box at the par-4 eleventh hole was moved back 35 yards prior to the 2002 tournament. (Courtesy of Michael O'Byrne Photography.)

Priceless!

With wholesale changes made to the Augusta National for the 2002 Masters, golfers now face a vastly different course than the one played during the first sixty-five years of the tournament. In fact, a good case could be made that the scoring record of 63 over the shorter pre-2002 Masters course shared by Nick Price and Greg Norman is dated. Price's record round occurred on the day prior to Jack Nicklaus' sixth green jacket in 1986. The round is also noteworthy because Price established a single-round mark of ten birdies and attained the feat despite a bogey at the first hole and a long birdie putt that lipped out at eighteen.

In October 1990, heavy rains dumped over a foot of water on Augusta in less than two days. The ensuing waters washed out numerous roads in Augusta as creeks overflowed their banks. Flooding along Rae's Creek caused problems in several areas of town including the Augusta National, where water flows between the historic eleventh, twelfth, and thirteenth greens at Amen Corner. The rushing water was so severe that the entire eleventh green, pond and adjoining dam, the front bunker at the twelfth hole, and the members tee box at thirteen were washed away. Damage was also sustained to the historic Hogan and Nelson Bridges. In the waters wake a deep chasm was gouged out at the spot where Amen Corner begins.

Utilizing topographic maps and new laser technology, a temporary eleventh green was rebuilt in its entirety by the end of Thanksgiving weekend. Unless they had seen the water damage for themselves, golfers would never have known the difference. At the conclusion of the 1991 Masters Tournament, the eleventh green was rebuilt permanently.

In October 1990, heavy rains dumped over a foot of water on Augusta in less than two days.

Opposite: Nick's Knack The day before Jack Nicklaus won his sixth green jacket in 1986, Nick Price established the new single round scoring record of 63, later tied by Greg Norman. Here Price prepares to tee it up during a rainy practice round prior to the 2001 Masters Tournament.

"With a new eleventh green in place for this year's Masters Tournament, officials say they will scrap the old course record book and begin anew this spring."

Nick Price remembers the flooding that year for a different reason. One of golf's greatest ambassadors, Price would soon be on the receiving end of an April Fools' joke that centered on the flooding. At the time, Price held the record for the best round (63) in Masters history. He currently shares this mark with his good friend Greg Norman.

In early March 1991, Augustan Steve Belcher and longtime WJBF-TV (Augusta ABC affiliate) Media Services Director Tom McManus schemed to play a practical joke on Price.

When the WJBF-TV 6 P.M. newscast concluded one fateful night in late March that year, McManus arranged for a special "Nick Price-cast" to be taped and craftily edited into the day's regular sportscast. No one in Augusta saw this edited production, only Price.

The newly edited and factually erroneous "Price-cast" went something like this: "Following their last-place finish in the National League West last season, the Atlanta Braves feel they are ready to wash away the past and finally be contenders this season (which actually turned out to be the case.) And in news from the Augusta National, it appears that recent flooding has also washed away all course records. With a new eleventh green in place for this year's Masters

Tournament, officials say they will scrap the old course record book and begin anew this spring."

"The record most affected by this decision is Nick Price's single-round mark of 63, which will be denoted in the books with an asterisk. A club official who declined to be named has even gone as far as saying that had the current green been in place in 1986, Price would never have been able to set the course record." Then after a short pause the tape concluded with "Happy April Fools' Day, Nick, from your friends at WJBF-TV. We'll see you at the Masters."

Several days later, the altered "Price-cast" on video-tape was delivered to Price's home in Orlando. Nick had been informed by Belcher that there was a story out of Augusta that he thought Price might be interested in viewing. The amiable Price, who has three majors to his credit but has been unable to deliver four consecutive solid rounds in Augusta, had no idea the content of the enclosed videotape.

Cost of a badge in 1986 to watch Nick Price set the Masters single-round scoring record? Seventy-five dollars.

Cost to repair the washed-out eleventh green at the Augusta National? Millions.

Cost to see Nick Price up off his couch, screaming "No, no, no!" at his television set? Priceless!

Nick Price — On establishing the new single-round Masters Tournament scoring record of 63.

"I made seven birdies through twelve holes and going down seventeen I was pumped up. But you never know what to do. You try and throttle back a little and try and not get too excited. Then you want a little bit of adrenaline to keep yourself up. You've got to try and find that medium and try to keep your pace as consistent as possible and try not to get too up or too down from it. I was really excited out there, so you kind of work against yourself sometimes. I am a very hyper person; I get excited a good deal. I just had so much fun out there today. Everyone was behind me coming in, and they wanted to see the record broken, and I wanted to break a record, and it was a great feeling. It was really a lot of fun."

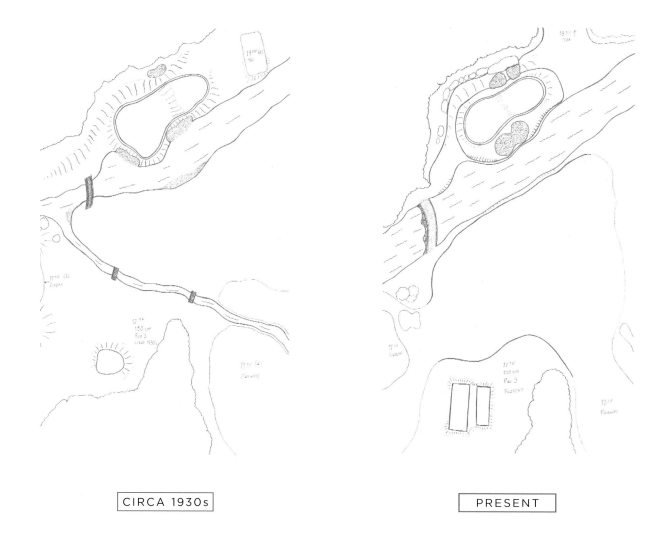

CIRCA 1930s

PRESENT

HOLE 12
Happiness and Heartbreak

MAJOR CHANGES

1951
Right side of green extended.

1958
Dedication of Ben Hogan Bridge.

1960
Putting surface raised.

1965
Tee box adjusted.

1981
Underside of putting surface fitted with heating and cooling system.

Hole 12, circa 1934 This shortest hole on the course has played a major role in determining the outcomes of numerous Masters Tournaments. In early tournament history golfers traversed the waters of Rae's Creek at the twelfth hole by a wooden footbridge that is barely visible to the far left of this photograph. (Photo by Tony Sheehan. Courtesy of Joseph M. Lee III.)

		GOLDEN BELL
par	3	
1934 yardage	150	
1959 yardage	155	
current yardage	155	
difficulty	2	

Twelfth Hole, circa 1950s View of the picturesque twelfth fairway and green during the 1950s. In early Masters history, a tributary to Rae's Creek also wound its way across the fairway. (Courtesy of Summerville Photo.)

Hole History

During course construction in 1932, a large amount of earth was required to be moved across Rae's Creek to build up the twelfth green. An old Native American burial ground was unearthed in the process and this is attributed by some for the many strange occurrences at the hole throughout Masters history. The hole was first known as the Three Pines hole.

The shortest par 3 at the Augusta National, the twelfth has played as one of the toughest and most critical in Masters history. For the 2004 Masters, it was ranked ninth. Just over 20 yards at its widest, the back-to-front sloped putting surface is guarded by Rae's Creek and a greenside bunker in front and two greenside bunkers strategically situated to the back of the putting surface. Coupled with swirling winds and the mystique of Amen Corner, hitting this long, narrow surface makes for one of the most compelling theaters in all of sport. In early Masters history, the tributary to Rae's Creek that runs alongside the thirteenth hole also extended across the twelfth and thirteenth fairways.

Memorable Moments

Likely the most popular hole in golf history, this signature hole at the Augusta National has proven the turning point in many Masters Tournament finishes.

"This is an interesting pitch shot to a long narrow green immediately over a stream. The bold player will go for the pin on the right, while the less ambitious will steer for the larger landing space on the left side of the green. There is a steep sandy bank covered with beautiful trees beyond the green."

—ALISTER MACKENZIE, 1932

For Arnold Palmer, the twelfth proved the decisive hole in back-to-back final round appearances (1958 and 1959), only one of which he would win. During Sunday's round in 1958, heading toward his first Masters victory, Palmer received a favorable ruling on his embedded golf ball.

Standing one-up on playing partner Ken Venturi to start the hole, Palmer hit a 7-iron off the tee to a spot between the putting surface and back bunkers, where the ball plugged in the soggy turf. When he discovered his sunken golf ball, Palmer promptly announced his intentions to take a free drop. But rules official Arthur Lacey interpreted the free-drop rule to include only golf balls in the fairway or on the green, neither of which applied to Palmer.

An incensed Palmer declared his intention to also play a second ball on appeal and let the Rules Committee decide his fate. He followed by advancing the plugged golf ball only a foot and a half, chipped onto the putting surface, and two putted for five. Then after a free drop, Palmer replayed the shot and chipped a second ball close enough to make par.

From that point on, Palmer's game caught fire and a bit of luck. Not yet knowing his fate at the twelfth, an inspired Palmer posted an eagle-three at thirteen. It was not until Palmer was playing the fifteenth hole that he was officially informed that his appeal had stood. He was awarded three at the twelfth. Coupled with his

View from Above Aerial photograph of the twelfth green at the Augusta National Golf Club. Note the Ben Hogan Bridge (left), the Byron Nelson Bridge (right), and the thirteenth tee box (upper right). Prior to the 2002 tournament, a small parcel of land was purchased from the adjacent Augusta Country Club and the Masters tees at the thirteenth hole were moved back 20–25 yards. (© Historic Golf Photos–Ron Watts Collection.)

Amen! The fairway and Ben Hogan Bridge leading to the twelfth green as it appeard in 1994. The shortest hole on the course, the par-3 twelfth has played as the second most difficult hole overall in Masters history. (Courtesy of Michael O'Byrne Photography.)

eagle at thirteen, the advantage to Palmer was four shots over the two holes and proved critical in the eventual outcome. Palmer would bogey the sixteenth, knock his tee shot off the trunk of Ike's tree at seventeen before salvaging par at the hole, and bogey eighteen. The shaky ending would leave Palmer with a one-shot margin of victory over Doug Ford and Fred Hawkins and his first green jacket.

In 1959, Palmer found the twelfth hole a challenge for the second straight year during final-round play. Leading by two going to the twelfth hole, he knocked his tee shot into Rae's Creek. Palmer emerged with a triple-bogey six, ultimately ending his bid for back-to-back Masters titles. The three extra shots at the twelfth hole proved crucial as Palmer finished in third place, two in back of that years' winner Art Wall.

Palmer's 1959 fate could easily have been replayed by Fred Couples in 1992, who came to the hole with a three-shot lead in the final round. How Couples' tee shot did not find water off the steep bank fronting the twelfth green remains a mystery. Couples' shot rolled back toward Rae's Creek but stopped just short of the water on the rain-soaked bank. From a side-hill stance and with his right foot on the edge of the water, he got up and down to save par. Couples held on to defeat Raymond Floyd by two shots. After the tournament Couples replayed his feelings: "I had, never been so nervous, never wanted to hit it where I hit it, but got a break of a lifetime, and obviously I took advantage of a big break."

In 2004, Phil Mickelson went on a Sunday back-nine birdie binge on his way to his first Masters title by a single shot over Ernie Els. A birdie at the twelfth hole got things started as Mickelson birdied five of the last seven holes. For Mickelson, it marked his seventh top-ten finish in the Masters in eleven appearances.

Highs and Lows

The toughest par 3 on the course, the twelfth hole has yielded just three holes in one during Masters Tournament competition: Claude Harmon in 1947, William Hyndman in 1959, and Curtis Strange in 1988.

Scott Verplank played the hole to near perfection during the 2003 Masters Tournament when he birdied the hole each round. Verplank's 2-2-2-2 is the lowest combined score on any one hole in Masters history.

Tom Weiskopf had a particularly tough time on the hole during the 1980 Masters, plunking five shots into Rae's Creek to record a record 13 on the hole. The next day, Weiskopf followed up by knocking two more golf balls into Rae's Creek before exiting the tournament with twenty shots taken at the twelfth hole in two rounds.

"The championship location for the pin here is in the shallow area of the green on the right. Here the distance must be gauged very accurately, and the wind sweeping down Rae's Creek is often deceptive to the player standing on the tee about to hit. The inclination here is to be well up, or at least to favor the left side where the green is somewhat wider. Once the tee shot has been played into the creek, the short pitch to the shallow green is terrifying indeed."

—BOBBY JONES, 1959

Rae's On The Right A rare early side view of the 12th hole putting green at the Augusta National Golf Club bordered by Rae's Creek. Note the wooden footbridge from the 13th tee in the background. (Courtesy of Western Golf Association.)

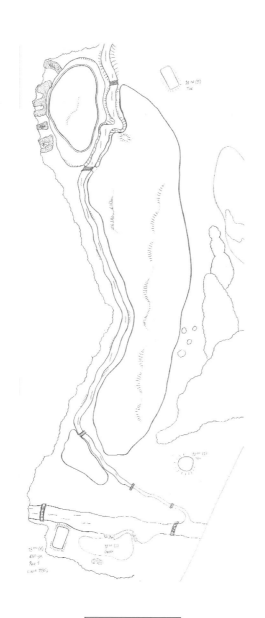

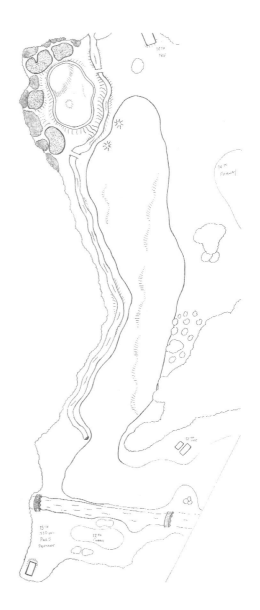

CIRCA 1930s

PRESENT

HOLE 13
Good Luck for Some

MAJOR CHANGES

1954
Contours on putting surface redirected and greenside bunker adjusted.

1958
Dedication of Byron Nelson Bridge.

1967
Tee box lengthened forward 5 yards.

1974
Tee box lengthened back 5 yards.

1975
Tee box lengthened back 7 additional yards.

1975
Putting surface redesigned.

1988
Left and back greenside swales reduced.

1994
Ventilation system installed at green.

1995
Creek fronting green altered.

2002
Tee box relocated 20–25 yards back.

Hole 13, circa 1934 Due to its natural setting along a tributary of Rae's Creek, this was the first hole that Alsiter MacKenzie and Bobby Jones decided upon when they walked the grounds of the old Fruitlands Nurseries in the summer of 1931. (Photo by Tony Sheehan. Courtesy of Joseph M. Lee III.)

		AZALEA
par	5	
1934 yardage	480	
1959 yardage	475	
current yardage	510	
difficulty	17	

"This is played along the course of a brook with the final shot finishing to a green over the stream with a background of a hill slope covered with pine trees. The hole has some of the best golfing features of the Seventeenth Hole at Cypress Point, California, and the ideal hole depicted in C. B. Macdonald's book."

—ALISTER MACKENZIE, 1932

Hole History

This par 5 dogleg-left is the first hole that Alister MacKenzie and Bobby Jones happened upon when designing the course in 1931. The hole is guarded by a tree line along its left side and a tributary to Rae's Creek that extends in front of the green; in early Masters history this tributary also ran across the thirteenth fairway, on the other side of Rae's Creek. Four massive rear greenside bunkers compliment a severe back-to-front sloped putting surface. With the acquisition of a small parcel of land from neighboring Augusta Country Club, a new back tee was installed prior to the 2002 Masters Tournament. This lengthened the hole by 25 yards and marked the biggest change to the thirteenth since the golf course opened.

Memorable Moments

Byron Nelson posted an eagle at the thirteenth hole in the final round of the 1937 tournament to overtake Ralph Guldahl and win the first of his two Masters titles. Coupled with a birdie at the twelfth hole, Nelson made up six shots as Guldahl took eleven shots over the two holes. Dedicated in 1958, the Byron Nelson Bridge spanning Rae's Creek at the thirteenth tee commemorates the achievement.

Jeff Maggert scored only the third double-eagle in Masters history and the first at the thirteenth hole during the final round of the 1994 Masters. Well out of contention, Maggert's feat was witnessed by few spectators as he holed a 3-iron from 222 yards.

For those that were on hand, Maggert recalled, "Everybody was yelling and screaming. I felt like I was in the lead or something." It was a great moment for

"It is a dogleg hole, played diagonally over a stream that constitutes a continuous hazard. The long hitter may go for as long a carry as he wishes and thus reach the green with a long second shot, but the less powerful driver can play out across the stream, play his second up the fairway and his third on the green without encountering any trouble. Here's another hole without a bunker."

—*NEW YORK TIMES, 1933*

Thirteenth Green, circa 1950s An early side view of the thirteenth green at the Augusta National Golf Club. Note the width of the tributary of Rae's Creek and the wooden footbridges that carried golfers from fairway to putting surfaces. (© Historic Golf Photos–Ron Watts Collection.)

Signature Setting, circa 1994 View of the picturesque thirteenth hole as it appeared in the mid-1990s. Byron Nelson scored an eagle at the hole to overtake leader Ralph Guldahl in the final round of the 1937 Masters. (Courtesy of Michael O'Byrne Photography.)

Maggert in an event he would otherwise likely as soon forget. Bogged down with an 82 on Saturday, Maggert finished in last place among those who made the cut.

It is here that Nick Faldo began his back-side Sunday charge in 1990 to tie Raymond Floyd at the end of regulation. Down by four shots with six holes to play, Faldo registered birdies at thirteen, fifteen, and sixteen to force a playoff with Floyd. Faldo won the ensuing sudden death playoff or a second straight year.

Highs and Lows

During the first round of the 1934 Masters, Jones hit his approach with a 3-wood to four feet, leaving him with a golden opportunity to post an eagle, but he missed the putt and settled for a tap-in birdie.

Playing in his first Masters in 1978, Tsuneyuki "Tommy" Nakajima of Japan found the par-5 thirteenth to be especially unlucky. His was such a comedy of errors that Nakajima actually lost count along the way to thirteen, as in thirteen shots. Two years later Tom Weiskopf joined Nakajima with the same score at the par-3 twelfth hole. Tommy and Tom's efforts remain the highest single-hole totals in Masters history.

Nakajima only wanted to make up for a bogey at the preceding twelfth hole during second-round play. "I promised myself to make an eagle," Nakajima later recanted, "but I tried too hard." Nakajima's journey started with a drive into the ditch that fronted the tee in the thirteenth fairway. Drop. Penalty shot. Then he followed a 5-iron to the fairway with an approach into the creek in front of the green. This is where Nakajima's nightmare really began. His shot from the creek went straight into the air. It also came back down straight, on his shoe, good for a two-stroke penalty. Undaunted, Nakajima handed the club to his caddie to be wiped off and in doing so it grazed the creek water. Grounding his club in a hazard: two-shot penalty. At this point, Nakajima had already taken more penalty strokes (5) than actual strokes (4). His ball still in the creek, his problems were not over yet. When the frustrated Nakajima finally hacked his way out of the creek, his ball flew the green into an awaiting bunker, his third hazard on the same hole. A pitch out of the sand and two putts later the odyssey was over. Nakajima had just spent a baker's dozen strokes on one hole. Was it an eleven or actually thirteen? Not one to quibble over a stroke or two Nakajima recounted and, sure enough, it was an unlucky thirteen. Had it not been for the gaffe Nakajima would have finished the day at even par, but a second straight 80 sent him packing.

"In my opinion this thirteenth hole is one of the finest holes for competitive play I have ever seen. The player is first tempted to dare the creek on his tee shot by playing in close to the corner, because if he attains this position he has not only shortened the hole but obtained a more level lie for his second shot. Driving out to the right not only increases the length of the second, but encounters an annoying sidehill lie. The second shot as well entails a momentous decision whether or not to try for the green. A player who dares the creek on either his first or second shot may very easily encounter a six or seven on this hole. Yet the reward of successful, bold play is most enticing."

—BOBBY JONES, 1959

Testing the Waters Two-time Masters champion (1980 and 1983) Seve Ballesteros heads into uncharted waters in front of the thirteenth green in 1989. Ballesteros finished in fifth place as Nick Faldo won his first green jacket. (Courtesy of Joe Dromsky Collection.)

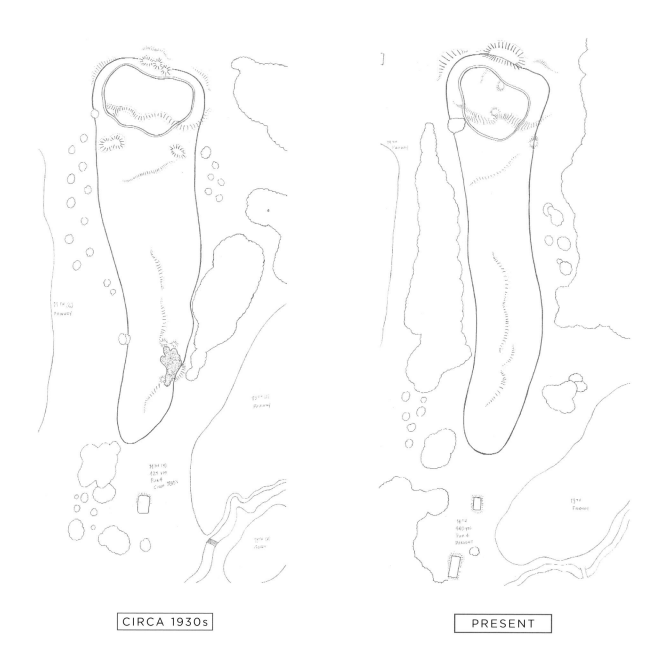

CIRCA 1930s

PRESENT

HOLE 14
No Day at the Beach

Hole 14, circa 1934
The original fourteenth hole designed by Alister MacKenzie included a fairway bunker that was removed in the early 1950s. Today it is the only hole at the Augusta National Golf Club without such a hazard. (Photo by Tony Sheehan. Courtesy of Joseph M. Lee III.)

MAJOR CHANGES

1952
Right-side fairway bunker removed.

1972
Tee box moved left.

1972
Apron of putting surface extended forward.

1974
New tee box.

1987
Putting surface altered to accommodate new pin placement to back left.

2002
Tee box relocated 30–35 yards back.

		CHINESE FIR
par	4	
1934 yardage	425	
1959 yardage	420	
current yardage	440	
difficulty	8	

Fourteen Scene The fourteenth fairway and well-hidden putting surface at Augusta National Golf Club as it appeared in 1948. (© Historic Golf Photos–Ron Watts Collection.)

"This hole embodies some of the features of the Sixth Hole at St. Andrews, Scotland. A long drive skirting or played over a bunker on the right will give a visible shot to the green. From the left the green is semi-blind and moreover a run up approach will be required over a succession of hillocks and hollows."

—ALISTER MACKENZIE, 1932

Hole History

This slight dogleg left is the only hole on the course without bunkers, but severe undulations on the putting surface more than make up for their absence. When the course first opened the fourteenth hole featured a fairway bunker, and the fifth, fifteenth, and seventeenth played without bunkers. A new tournament tee installed prior to the 2002 Masters added a much-needed 35 yards in length to the hole. Originally known as the Spanish Dagger hole, it has since been changed to Chinese Fir.

Memorable Moments

During the final round of the epic 1986 Masters, Greg Norman posted the first of four consecutive backside birdies that brought him to the seventy-second hole in need of just par to tie Jack Nicklaus and send the tournament into a playoff. Playing in the group in back of Nicklaus that afternoon and one ahead of the

"The most popular line off the tee is slightly to left of center to gain the crest of the hill and not risk the runoff of the fairway to the right. A slight deviation to left of this line often encounters the upper branches of the group of pine trees on this side. The green is quite large and with many interesting and difficult contours. The putting surface along the front of the green spills over the contours into the fairway. But an approach putt from this area is exceedingly difficult. A really good second shot leaving the ball close to the hole is most comforting here."

—BOBBY JONES, 1959

Seve Ballesteros–Tom Kite combination, Norman joined in a classic showdown for the green jacket.

Jack Nicklaus recalled the showdown: "As I got to the fourteenth tee I looked up at the leaderboard, and there's only two fellows in front of me, I was seven [under par], Ballesteros was nine, and Kite was eight. I said there's only two guys in front of me I've got to beat now, as long as I keep playing. I eagled fifteen. I got to the leaderboard and Seve was the only guy in front of me. I said okay, he's got a little bit more golf to play, and you know, just keep playing, if you can make yourself a birdie or two you just might do something. And by gosh, I almost made a hole-in-one at sixteen and I made birdie at seventeen. So he had his work cut out for him, and of course it wasn't Seve who turned out being the guy that could tie me." (With a birdie at seventeen, Greg Norman would tie Nicklaus for the lead, but a bogey at eighteen would cost him a chance at forcing a playoff.)

"The fans were fantastic, they really started getting to me. And as far as, you know, [I] start welling up, and I start saying gosh, you know, this is exciting, and it's great to have that kind of support, the people are just fantastic. But I kept telling myself, hey Jack, you've got some golf to play, let's sort of settle yourself back down. And, but to be through an experience like that, as nice as the people were, it was just something that you remember all your life."

Highs and Lows

Two-time Masters champion (1985 and 1993) Bernhard Langer birdied this hole during all four rounds of the 1991 Masters Tournament. Unguarded by bunkers, the hole has yielded fourteen eagles in tournament play, the most of any Augusta National par-4 design.

Co-single round scoring holder Nick Price, who recorded a 63 in 1986, also holds the distinction of the highest score ever posted at the hole with an eight in 1993.

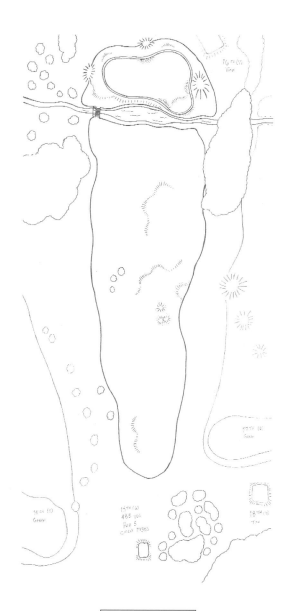

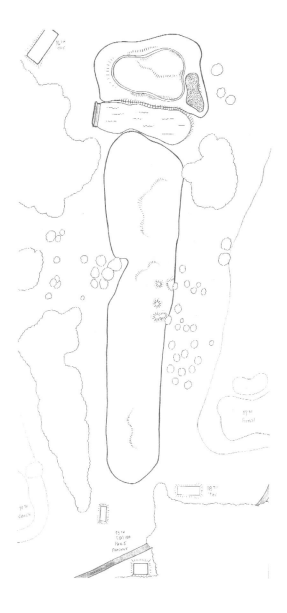

CIRCA 1930s

PRESENT

HOLE 15
Sarazen's Showcase

Hole 15, circa 1934 View of the fifteenth green that Gene Sarazen faced as he made the double-eagle "heard 'round the world" in 1935. Bobby Jones was among the small gallery who actually witnessed the feat. (Photo by Tony Sheehan. Courtesy of Joseph M. Lee III.)

MAJOR CHANGES

1955
Dedication of Gene Sarazen Bridge.

1957
Addition of right-front greenside bunker.

1961
Pond fronting green enlarged.

1963
Back greenside mound removed and right greenside mound lengthened.

1964
Right greenside bunker enlarged.

1969
Tee box moved back and right.

1969
Mounds added to right-side fairway.

1999
Pine trees added to right- and left-side fairway.

1999
Right-side fairway mounds graded down.

par	5	
1934 yardage	485	**FIRETHORN**
1959 yardage	520	
current yardage	500	
difficulty	18	

Fifteenth Green, circa 1948 The fifteenth green at Augusta National Golf Club prior to enlargement of the pond guarding the putting surface. (© Historic Golf Photos–Ron Watts Collection.)

Hole History

The easiest hole throughout the course of Masters Tournament history, the par-5 fifteenth was the site of one of the greatest golf shots of all time. Originally designed by Alister MacKenzie to play 485 yards, the hole now plays just 15 yards longer. Water to the front and a right greenside bunker guard this final par-5 test at the Augusta National. Early in Masters Tournament history, the lone hazard standing guard over the putting surface was a narrow pond that fronted the hole. It was later expanded into the much larger pond that golfers face today in their quest to reach the green.

Advances in equipment have necessitated efforts at

"This is a three-shot hole to most golfers. It is not only an interesting three-shot hole, as one will be maneuvering for position from the tee shot onwards, but also a magnificent tee shot hole as a skillful and courageous player will, aided by a large hillock to the right, be able to pull his second shot around to the green. A pond in front of the green provides the penalty for the long player who fails to make a perfect second shot."

—ALISTER MACKENZIE, 1932

tightening the design on this part of the course, earlier with mounds and more recently with trees. The mounds were rendered obsolete when technology progressed to the point that players routinely carried them with their drives. A right-side tree line was established between the fifteenth and seventeenth fairways in 1999 to replace the mounds, but produce a similar effect—to deter players from bailing out to the right where they had an open shot to the green in two.

Memorable Moments

The 1935 Masters was contested with the nines reverted to MacKenzie and Bobby Jones' original design. As Gene Sarazen made ready for his tee shot at the fifteenth hole, Craig Wood held the clubhouse lead at 6-under par and was already being heralded as the new Masters Champion. Jones, too, had finished his round and made his way to follow the exploits of the next to last grouping that day, Sarazen and playing partner Walter Hagen. In the closing hour of play in Sunday's final round the scene would shift dramatically. Jones was one of less than two dozen spectators to actually witness the drama that was about to unfold.

Three shots in back of Wood, Sarazen did not care for the lie staring back at him on the fifteenth fairway. With time running out, he pulled from his bag a utility club of his own invention. The newly designed "Wilson Turf Rider" 4-wood was made specially to hit from such a tight lie and get the ball airborne quickly.

In an effort to muster every ounce of strength from his tiny frame and carry the then small creek fronting the green, Sarazen shifted the ball back in his stance and let go with a swing that would change the course of golf history. From the instant he made contact, he sensed there was something magical about the way the ball felt when it left the clubface. Jones later wrote of Sarazen's shot, "His swing into the ball was so perfect and so free, one knew immediately it was a gorgeous shot."

Now certain that the low trajectory missile would clear the water, Sarazen focused on the ball and bounded down the fairway in fast pursuit. When he saw the ball hit in front of the green and kick slightly left toward the hole, he was just hoping it would land somewhere close to the pin. Straining to follow the path of his golf ball as it inched toward the cup, what happened next was a blur. When twenty-two greenside spectators erupted, it confirmed what Sarazen would

Fifteenth Fairway, circa 1994 View of the fifteenth pond and fairway at the Augusta National Golf Club, the final par-5 test on the course. Though it has played the easiest of any hole on the course over time, the fifteenth has also wreaked havoc on the bids of many would-be champions. (Courtesy of Michael O'Byrne Photography.)

"Here again we see boldness and accuracy rewarded. The design of the hole gives assistance to the big hitter who has driven far and accurately, for the large hillock has been built to the right of the loop of the stream which assists him in pulling his second shot around to the green. The hole has certain characteristics of the first hole at St. Andrews."

—*NEW YORK TIMES, 1933*

not dare let himself suspect, that his golf ball had somehow found its way to the bottom of the cup.

Against all odds, Sarazen had made up three shots with one swing of the club to pull even with Wood and set the stage for a thirty-six-hole playoff the following day. Winning Monday's daylong playoff by five shots, Sarazen completed a career Grand Slam and added the seventh and final major to his résumé. More importantly, his "shot heard 'round the world" helped cement Jones' tournament in the nation's consciousness and seemed to emphasize that the course was now back again in its rightful playing order. It was as if MacKenzie himself somehow orchestrated one final touch of artistry to confirm his approval of Jones' reversal of the nines. The Augusta National was back to the order that they originally envisioned during their first walks along the property in July 1931.

For his part, Sarazen was rather fond of the double-eagle and inquired of his caddie Thor "Stovepipe" Nordwall if he had overheard any talk of a marker to commemorate the shot. According to Ward Clayton's book, *Men on the Bag, The Caddies of Augusta National*, Stovepipe replied, "Mister Gene, they went down there this morning, some of the greenskeepers, I mean, and they done sprinkled a little rye seed in the divot and covered it up." Twenty years later, Sarazen finally got

his marker in the form of a bridge over the pond to the left side of the green. The Sarazen Bridge was dedicated during Masters Week 1955.

Highs and Lows

While Gene Sarazen's two is the lowest score recorded at the fifteenth hole, Masashi "Jumbo" Ozaki (1987), Ben Crenshaw (1997), and Ignacio Garrido (1998) have each posted record high elevens on the hole.

The finish of the 1986 Masters Tournament best captures the high and low points of this final par 5 at the Augusta National. It was in the closing round of the event that the second-best shot in Masters history was recorded at the fifteenth hole. This time a much larger gallery and worldwide television audience would witness the happening.

By the time he reached his drive in the fifteenth fairway that afternoon, Jack Nicklaus stood four shots in back of Seve Ballesteros, who had moments earlier posted an eagle at the nearby par-5 thirteenth hole. Ballesteros was paired with perennial runner-up Tom Kite, who was also intent on making a challenge for the green jacket.

Fifty-one years after Gene Sarazen pulled the "Turf Rider" utility 4-wood from his bag in the 1935

"The fairway of this hole is quite wide. The short rough on the left is far removed from the line of play and there is no demarcation on the right between the fairway of the fifteenth and that of the seventeenth. The tee shot may be hit almost anywhere without encountering trouble. This fairway, being on high ground, usually provides more run to the ball than most other holes of the course. The design of the green causes it to be most receptive to a second shot played from the right-center of the fairway. The greater depth of the putting surface is on the right side. The left side is quite shallow, considering the length of the second shot."

—BOBBY JONES, 1959

Masters, Nicklaus chose a 4-iron in his quest for an unprecedented sixth green jacket. Nicklaus' answer to Ballesteros was an approach shot that nearly flew into the hole as a stunned gallery lifted a deafening roar in response. Moments later when his 12-foot eagle putt dropped, the ensuing roar shook Augusta and reverberated throughout the golf world: Jack was back!

Before Ballesteros had time to hit his own approach shot from the fifteenth fairway, the gallery erupted once more; Nicklaus had birdied the sixteenth hole and now trailed the leader by a single shot.

With momentum shifted decidedly in Nicklaus' favor, Ballesteros watched in horror as his own approach shot to fifteen found the pond in front of the green. A shell-shocked Ballesteros saw his lead evaporate with a bogey as Nicklaus stalked seventeen. In the time it had taken to play a hole and a half, Nicklaus had cut three shots from Ballesteros' lead. In the same

stretch going forward, Ballesteros trailed Master Jack for good. Kite missed an eagle opportunity at the fifteenth, but his birdie putt brought him to 8-under par. For the moment at least, Kite had pulled even with Nicklaus and Ballesteros.

Playing in the final pairing of the day directly in back of Ballesteros and Kite, Greg Norman was also making noise. "The Shark" posted four consecutive birdies on the fourteenth through seventeenth holes that tied him with Nicklaus at 9-under par (Jack also birdied seventeen). Another birdie by Norman and he would have won the tournament outright; with par he would have forced a playoff with Nicklaus. But an errant approach shot at the eighteenth led to a bogey for Norman and a second-place finish. At age forty-six, Nicklaus had roared past fourteen golfers either ahead of or tied with him at the start of the day to win his sixth green jacket.

Sarazen Special, circa 1990 Gene Sarazen, 1935 champion, acknowledges the accolades of Masters patrons. Sarazen's double-eagle at the fifteenth hole in the closing moments of the 1935 tournament bouyed his charge to victory and helped put the Masters on the map. (Courtesy of Joe Dromsky Collection.)

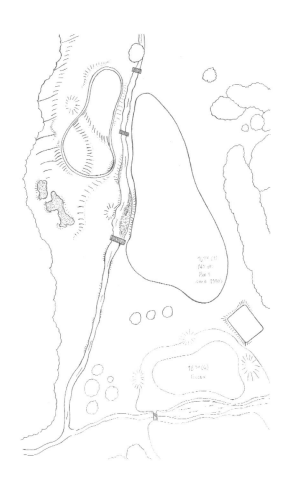

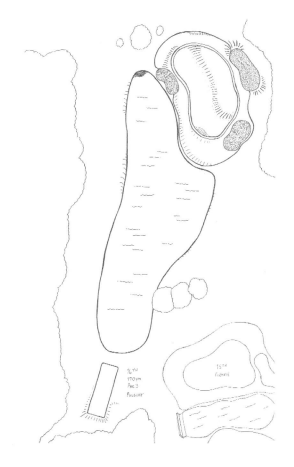

CIRCA 1930s

PRESENT

HOLE 16
Premium Putts

Hole 16, circa 1934 A rare early view at the original sixteenth hole that was designed by Alister MacKenzie to play over a tributary of Rae's Creek. Bobby Jones later sketched the hole to play longer and entirely over water. (Photo by Tony Sheehan. Courtesy of Joseph M. Lee III.)

MAJOR CHANGES

1946
New green constructed.

1947
Stream transformed into pond.

1947
Putting surface shifted right.

1947
Tee box relocated left.

1961
Tee box lengthened and relocated left.

1966
Small section of pond and area to left and back of green filled in.

1973
Section on left side of pond filled in.

par	3
1934 yardage	145
1959 yardage	190
current yardage	170
difficulty	9

REDBUD

Number 16, circa 1940 Early view of the original sixteenth green at Augusta. Directly in back of the green (upper left) is the hill leading from the sixth hole tee box. (© Historic Golf Photos–Ron Watts Collection.)

Hole History

The original hole designed by Alister MacKenzie played just 145 yards. It was guarded by the same tributary of Rae's Creek that runs along and in front of the thirteenth green, featured a mound in the center of a shallow putting surface, and had greenside bunkers in back. Initially the tee was located back right of the fifteenth green and shortly thereafter an alternate tee was added beyond the back-left side of the fifteenth putting surface.

"This is a somewhat similar hole over a stream to the best hole (seventh) at Stoke Poges, England. It is probably a better hole than the one at Stoke Poges as the green is more visible and the background more attractive."

—ALISTER MACKENZIE, 1932

In the late 1940s Bobby Jones sketched out an idea he had for a new design at the hole, which featured a new tee farther left and a pond. Then he turned the project over to architect Robert Trent Jones Sr. The result was a dramatically different design that transformed this par 3 into a difficult challenge. The new sixteenth hole was packed with 25 yards of additional length, three strategically located greenside bunkers, a challenging two-tiered green, and played entirely over water.

The left edge of the current pond at Number 16 draws an approximate outline of the creek that once fronted the original green. Spectators now congregate on the approximate area where the old bunkers were once located, on the hill overlooking the left side of the green.

Memorable Moments

With his tee shot 40 feet from the hole on the upper-right tier of sixteenth green, Jack Nicklaus watched as the 1975 Masters unfolded around him. From his vantage point at the sixteenth tee box he witnessed Johnny Miller and Tom Weiskopf birdie the fifteenth hole in the final round of the classic tournament. Weiskopf's birdie enabled him to maintain a one-shot lead on Nicklaus, who was now just one up on the hard charging Miller. Not to be outdone, Nicklaus answered moments later with a birdie putt of his own that left bear tracks in its wake. This time it was Weiskopf and Miller watching from the sixteenth tee

as Nicklaus pranced the putting surface and the gallery thundered with one of the loudest roars in Masters history. The birdie putt momentarily pulled Nicklaus into a tie for the lead and tilted the tournament back in his favor. When a shaken Weiskopf bogeyed the sixteenth, it proved a two-shot swing and one-shot lead for Nicklaus, all he would need to win his fifth green jacket.

The sixteenth hole also marks the start of Arnold Palmer's 3-3-3 close to win the 1960 Masters Tournament by one shot over Ken Venturi. While Palmer led from start to finish in regulation, it does not begin to describe how close the tournament really was. Down by one shot to start the final nine holes, Palmer squandered opportunities at the par-5 thirteenth and fifteenth holes to remain one shot back.

A brief encounter at the fifteenth green with caddie Nathaniel "Iron Man" Avery may have paved the way for Palmer's reversal of fortunes. In frustration over a poorly played wedge shot, which cost him another birdie opportunity, Palmer tossed his club in Avery's direction. It was a moment neither would forget. "Iron Man" responded, "Mr. Palmer, are we chokin'?" Palmer regained his composure over the final three holes. With Iron Man's remark ringing in his ears, Palmer made a tap-in par at the sixteenth and birdied the seventeenth and eighteenth holes to win the tournament by one shot.

Two years later, Palmer would mount another final-round comeback at the sixteenth hole to force a

Sixteenth Side, circa 1994 The original sixteenth green is now a favorite gathering spot for patrons to overlook Masters competition on the far side of the man-made pond. (Courtesy of Michael O'Byrne Photography.)

playoff with Gary Player and Dow Finsterwald. The following day Palmer won his third green jacket.

Highs and Lows

There have been nine holes-in-one at the par-3 sixteenth in Masters Tournament history, three of those by amateurs including Ross Sommerville's ace in the 1934 Masters. The Invitation Sommerville's mashie-niblick shot from 145 yards out was the first Tournament's hole-in-one. The following year, Willie Goggin hit a spade-mashie the same distance for his ace. The decade of the 1940s began and ended with two more amateurs making their marks at the sixteenth hole; Ray Billows aced the hole on the fly with an

"The pond extends from the front of the tee very nearly to the edge of the green. The contours of the green are such that several pin locations can be found along the left side close to the bunker and the pond. This is also the low side, so that a tee shot played for the middle of the putting surface, but with a slight draw, can be made to curl down toward the hole. Apart from the visible hazards on this hole, the player who leaves his ball on the forward area of the green with the pin near the back can have quite a problem getting down in two putts."

—BOBBY JONES, 1959

8-iron in the 1940 tournament, and John Dawson scored a hole-in-one with a 4-iron from 190 yards out in 1949. There have been five aces recorded at the hole since its redesign in 1947 to play over water. Clive Clark needed a 2-iron to ace the hole from 190 yards in 1968, while Corey Pavin used an 8-iron from 140 yards to accomplish the feat in 1992. Raymond Floyd scored his hole-in-one here in 1996 using a 5-iron from 182 yards. Playing in back-to-back groups during the final round of the 2004 Masters, Padraig Harrington and Kirk Triplett added their names to the record books with aces at the sixteenth hole.

In 1950 Herman Barron did not ace the hole, but recorded a pair of ones, next to each other. Played over the pond in 1950, the hole proved challenging for Barron who left with a record high eleven on his scorecard.

Among the leaders during the 1986 Masters tournament, the fifteenth and sixteenth holes proved to be a roller-coaster ride for Corey Pavin. During the third and fourth rounds of that tournament, Pavin rode the high of an eagle at fifteen to the low of double-bogey at sixteen to dash his hopes.

At Water's Edge Three-time champion Nick Faldo walks along the pond leading to the sixteenth green. The gallery lines the left side of the pond at the Augusta National Golf Club. Note the fringe surrounding the fifteenth green in the lower right corner of the photo. (Courtesy of Michael O'Byrne Photography.)

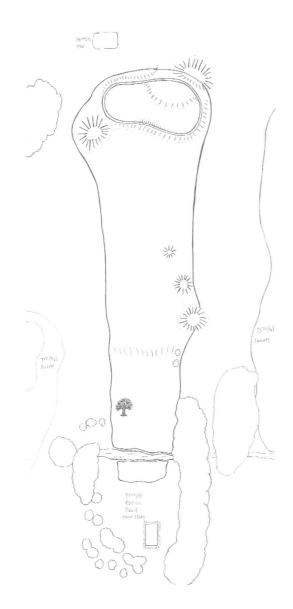

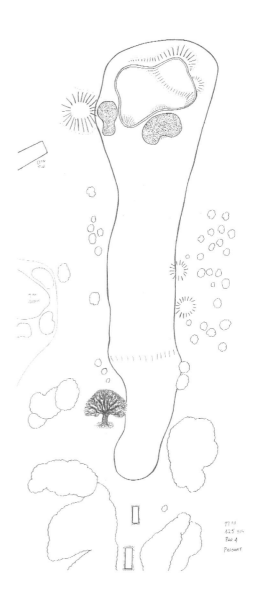

CIRCA 1930s

PRESENT

HOLE 17
Ike's Alibi

Hole 17, circa 1934 Early view of the seventeenth hole as it played without front greenside bunkers that were added some time between 1938 and 1948. Note the large mound to the left side of the putting surface that typified Alister MacKenzie's design at the Augusta National Golf Club. (Photo by Tony Sheehan. Courtesy of Joseph M. Lee III.)

MAJOR CHANGES

1940s
Greenside bunkers added.

1951
Ditch in front of tee box filled in and tee box lengthened forward 10 yards.

1972
Tee box moved back 10 yards.

1999
Tee box moved back 25 additional yards.

par	4	
1934 yardage	400	
1959 yardage	400	NANDINA
current yardage	425	
difficulty	10	

Seventeen Spectacular The seventeenth fairway and green at the Augusta National Golf Club as it appeared in 1948. Note the signature MacKenzie fairway undulations and mounds guarding the putting surface. (© Historic Golf Photos–Ron Watts Collection.)

"The construction of this green is somewhat similar to the famous Fourteenth at St. Andrews (reversed). It will be necessary to attack the green from the right and it will be essential to play a run-up shot if par figures are desired. We hope to make the turf of such a character that an indifferent pitch will not stop on the green. Until players have learned to play the desired shot this will undoubtedly be one of the most fiercely criticized holes."

—ALISTER MACKENZIE, 1932

Hole History

This short but uphill par 4 was originally designed to play 400 yards without bunkers. It features the "Eisenhower Pine" in its left-center fairway. A nemesis of former president Dwight D. Eisenhower, who also twice chaired the Club's Board of Governors, he once voiced his opinion to have the pine tree removed. This recommendation was ignored. The hole was lengthened an additional 25 yards in 1999 and the tree line bolstered on each side of the fairway. Ike's tree now causes grief for the Masters field each spring. A large, intricate putting surface is now guarded by front bunkers to the right and left.

Memorable Moments

It is now a moment suspended in time, etched in our memories forever: Jack Nicklaus crouching slightly, tongue peeking out, eyes afire, putter aloft, coaxing the "putt heard 'round the world." During the final round of the classic 1986 Masters, Nicklaus had gone from four shots down to even with Seve Ballesteros in the span of less than three holes. When his approach shot found the green at seventeen, the Golden Bear had set the stage for his sixth green jacket. With the gallery whipped into a frenzy and the script in place for a

During the final round of the 1968 tournament, Roberto De Vicenzo struck his birdie putt at seventeen just moments prior to Bob Goalby's eagle attempt at fifteen.

storybook ending, the forty-six-year-old Nicklaus did not disappoint. Greg Norman followed Nicklaus that day with a birdie at the seventeenth hole, his fourth in a row to tie Master Jack. Each was met with thundering ovations. But a bogey at eighteen would leave Norman one shot short of his goal.

Twenty-eight years earlier than Nicklaus' closing-round putt to seal his sixth green jacket, a young Arnold Palmer scrambled to win his first Masters. After a favorable ruling from play at the twelfth hole during the 1958 Tournament, Palmer also received a fortuitous kick off "Ike's Tree" in the seventeenth fairway during his final round. Leading by one shot, Palmer hooked his drive off the trunk of the tree, and it bounced back to the center of the fairway. Palmer managed to par the hole and hold on for his first Masters victory.

Highs and Lows

During the final round of the 1968 tournament, Roberto De Vicenzo struck his birdie putt at seventeen just moments prior to Bob Goalby's eagle attempt at fifteen. When De Vicenzo's putt fell, it gave him a short-lived two-shot lead. But when Goalby's putt seconds later also found the bottom of the cup, the

"The pine tree in the fairway, although only a little more than a hundred yards from the tee, has grown to such proportions that it provides a real menace to the tee shot. The proper line of play is to the right of this tree, but also to the left of the big mound and two other trees at the top of the hill. Depending upon the wind, a fine drive may leave a second shot of anything from a good 5-iron to a short pitch."

—BOBBY JONES, 1959

tournament was tied. In the ensuing commotion, Tommy Aaron scratched a four instead of three next to playing companion De Vicenzo's name on the scorecard. It did not help that De Vincenzo three-putted the final hole. Had he posted a par at the eighteenth, he would have tied Lloyd Mangrum's long-standing single-round scoring mark of 64. When De Vicenzo signed the incorrect scorecard after regulation play, the green jacket was awarded to Goalby.

On his forty-fifth birthday, Easter Sunday 1968, De Vicenzo was gracious in defeat as he addressed the media. "It was my fault," he remarked in his heavy Argentinean accent. "I play golf maybe thirty year all over the world and I am never wrong on my card. I think how stupid I am to do such a thing in this wonderful tournament. I want to congratulate Bob Goalby who play such fine golf. I think maybe he give me so much pressure on last few holes I lose my brains."

Fourteen golfers share the record high score of seven on this hole. Doug Ford, 1957 champion, has equaled the mark on two occasions (1995 and '97). The seventeenth hole has yielded just three eagles in tournament play, the latest by Davis Love III in 1998. Takaaki Kono scored the first eagle at the hole in 1969, and Tommy Nakajima posted a two on his scorecard here in 1989.

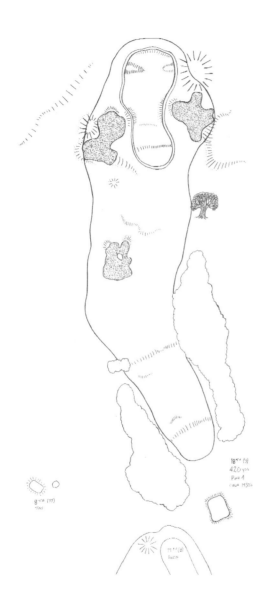

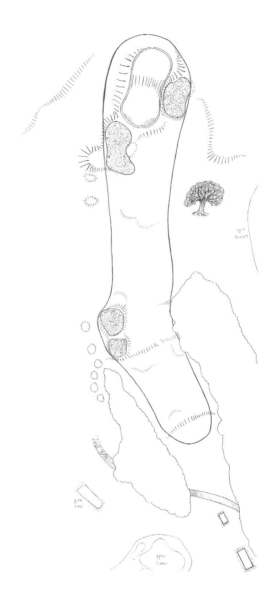

CIRCA 1930s

PRESENT

HOLE 18
At Center Stage

Hole 18, circa 1934 During the 1934 tournament this hole served as the closing test to the front nine. MacKenzie's original design featured a lone left-side bunker that ran along the lower half of the putting surface. (Photo by Tony Sheehan. Courtesy of Joseph M. Lee III.)

MAJOR CHANGES

1958
Spectator mounds to the left of green established.

1967
Left-side fairway hazard redesigned to include double bunker.

2002
Tee box moved back 55–60 yards and 5 yards right.

2002
Left fairway bunkers rearranged and enlarged slightly, and new trees set in place to the left of bunkers.

2002
Putting surface redone.

par	4
1934 yardage	420
1959 yardage	420
current yardage	465
difficulty	6

HOLLY

Close Quarters, circa 1947 Patrons gather around the eighteenth green at the Augusta National Golf Club for a closer look at the competition. Note the "Crow's Nest" atop the clubhouse to the upper left of the greenside bunker. (© Historic Golf Photos–Ron Watts Collection.)

Hole History

The sixth hardest hole in Masters history, the eighteenth played as the second toughest during the 2004 event when Phil Mickelson posted birdie to win the event at the seventy-second hole. This uphill, dogleg par 4 features a two-tiered putting surface twice as long (107 feet) as it is wide (50 feet). This closing hole to the first major of the golf season stands protected to the front left and right center by greenside bunkers. The eighteenth saw its first major change during the 1967 Masters when left fairway bunkers were added to combat an increase in driving distance, particularly by

Jack Nicklaus. For the 2002 tournament, a back tee was installed, adding an additional 45 yards in length. Golfers now face a challenging tee shot through a long chute of pines guarding the fairway right and left.

Memorable Moments

The eighteenth hole is famous for moments indelibly etched into a vast collection of Masters memories: Nicklaus' journey up the eighteenth fairway to ovation en route to winning his sixth green jacket in 1986; Tiger Woods' joyous arm motion following a tournament record 270 and his first Masters title in

"The tee shot is played over a valley and a bank running diagonally from left to right. The longer the drive to the right the easier the second shot, as the approach to the green is bunkered heavily on the left."

—ALISTER MACKENZIE, 1932

1997; Ben Crenshaw buckled over in emotion after his victory in the 1995 Masters, the same week his mentor, Harvey Penick, passed away. Crenshaw reflected on the day: "I enjoy playing this course so much, and I think experience helped me get around the golf course today. And I took what the golf course gave me today. I had some trying moments as all Masters Champions do, but plain and simple, I was luckier than the rest, and I really, honestly believe that fate has a great hand in winning this coat." An ecstatic Phil Mickelson leapt to new heights upon realizing his first major in the 2004 Masters.

The closing round of the 1975 Masters between Jack Nicklaus, Tom Weiskopf, and Johnny Miller came down to a classic seventy-second-hole showdown. A Nicklaus birdie–Weiskopf bogey at sixteen gave Master Jack a one-shot lead. As Nicklaus eyed his birdie attempt at the eighteenth green, he felt the roar as Miller's birdie attempt found the bottom of the cup at seventeen. Nicklaus waited at the eighteenth hole until he was assured that it was Miller and not Weiskopf who had hit the putt.

Nicklaus followed with a two-putt par and a scant one-shot lead. Though he earlier said he would not hit driver at eighteen feeling it would bring the bunkers into play, Weiskopf now had no choice. Weiskopf crushed his tee shot to within 110 yards from the hole, a drive that he would later describe as "the best I ever hit in my life, bar none." Miller first, then Weiskopf

responded with approach shots that landed safely on the putting surface within birdie range. With Nicklaus peeking out of the scorer's tent, the duo missed their birdie opportunities and Nicklaus emerged with his fifth green jacket. Miller was just happy to have been involved in the historic showdown, but for Weiskopf the defeat was devastating. "The nineteen seventy-five Masters, that was the end of me… I don't think I ever really recovered," Weiskopf remarked years later.

Highs and Lows

A showcase of history, the eighteenth hole at Alister MacKenzie's masterpiece is remembered equally for the heartbreak it has dealt: Arnold Palmer's double-bogey to finish one shot back in the 1961 Masters; Roberto De Vicenzo's incorrect scorecard in 1968; Greg Norman's bogey to end one shot behind Nicklaus in 1986.

The hole has yielded four eagles in Masters history, including John Huston's shot over the pines from the tenth fairway that gave him a share of the first-round lead in 1997. Felice Torza was the first golfer to eagle the hole in 1962. Jim Colbert posted a two on his scorecard at the finishing hole in 1974, while Dennis Hutchinson holed his approach shot in 1962. Five competitors have posted an eight on their scorecards to finish their rounds.

Compiling the ringer rounds (the highest and lowest scores posted on each individual hole) throughout Masters Tournament history produces a high ringer

Bird's Eye View Aerial view of patrons walking up the eighteenth fairway toward the green during the 1947 Masters Tournament. Jimmy Demaret won the event by two shots on Byron Nelson and in doing so became the first Masters champion to post below-par scores in all four rounds. (© Historic Golf Photos–Ron Watts Collection.)

round of 164 (76 on the front and a whopping 88 on the back side) with a paltry 33 as a low ringer total (17 shots on the front and 16 to complete the back side). In 1956 Charles Kunkle Jr. scored the highest over the eighteen holes when he posted a closing round 95 in extremely windy conditions.

The most contrasting start in Tournament history is owned by Craig Wood, who finished second in the first two Invitation Tournaments, then promptly opened the 1936 event with an 88. Though he was twenty-one shots better the next day at 67, Wood's score ballooned again with a closing round 76 and he ended fifteen shots out of first place. Had he played to even par 72 on the first and last days of the event, he would have beaten that years' winner, Horton Smith, by five shots. Five years later in 1941, Wood made good in winning the Masters.

"This hole is a slight dogleg to the right, the bend in the fairway coming at the top of the hill which can just about be carried by a fine tee shot. The bunker at the left front of the green causes it to be of some importance to drive close to the trees up the right side of the fairway, or even, if possible, to bend the tee shot a bit around the corner. The eighteenth green is quite long. The rear one-quarter of the putting surface embraces a plateau area which is often used as a pin location. The great difficulty here is to be up without going over. A second shot played into the slope in the middle of the green either stops or rolls back, so that the ensuing putt is difficult indeed."

—BOBBY JONES, 1959

The Final Stage View of the eighteenth green and fairway during a mid-1990s practice round. Major changes to the hole prior to the 2002 tournament included lengthening the hole 45 yards. (Courtesy of Michael O'Byrne Photography.)

The 19th Hole

Additional Artisans

Alister MacKenzie

Laid out the original eighteen holes in 1931 with associate Bobby Jones.

Bobby Jones

MacKenzie associate in laying out the original design.

Redesigned the sixteenth hole in 1947 to include a pond before turning the project over to Robert Trent Jones Sr.

Clifford Roberts

Had a hand in numerous course changes beginning with the ninth fairway landing area to accommodate his drives when the course was being constructed in 1932.

Had mounds to left side of the eighth green removed in 1956.

Suggested that the tenth tee box be moved far left in 1950.

Aided George W. Cobb in the design of the Par-3 Course.

Perry Maxwell

MacKenzie associate redesigned a new seventh green to include five bunkers and a new elevated tenth green as the first major changes to the course in 1937.

George W. Cobb

Redesigned the eighth green in 1956.

Designed the Par-3 Course with input from Clifford Roberts.

Robert Trent Jones Sr.

Constructed a new sixteenth hole designed by Bobby Jones to play over water in 1947.

Reconstructed the eleventh hole with a new tee box, fairway, and pond in 1950.

Joe Finger

Reconstructed the eighth green to original MacKenzie design specifications in 1979 with the left greenside mounds replaced.

George Fazio

Made numerous alterations to the course in the 1960s and '70s, under the watchful eye of Clifford Roberts, affecting the first, seventh, ninth, tenth, fourteenth, seventeenth, and eighteenth holes in varying degrees.

Tom Fazio

Designed two additional holes on the Par-3 Course to be played over Ike's Pond in 1986.

Performed alterations to holes 2, 11, 15, and 17 in 1998.

Performed major renovation project to nine holes prior to the 2002 Masters.

Jack Nicklaus

The six-time Masters champion provided architectural expertise for changes to the third and thirteenth holes.

Horton Smith

Winner of two of the first three Invitation Tournaments, Smith made suggestions to change the par-4 seventh hole that included lengthening and the replacement of five bunkers to surround the putting surface.

Ben Hogan

The bunker to the right side of the par-5 fifteenth green is courtesy of Hogan's suggestion in 1957 to add more strategy to the hole.

Byron Nelson

Oversaw reconstruction of mounding to the left side of the eighth green in 1979.

Entrance Drive The trees along Magnolia Lane were approximately seventy-five years old when the first Augusta National Invitation Tournament took place in 1934. (Photo by Tony Sheehan. Courtesy of Joseph M. Lee III.)

Monuments at MacKenzie's Place

The Augusta National Golf Club remains a testament to the artistry of codesigners Alister MacKenzie and Bobby Jones, and landmarks situated throughout the course honor those who have impacted the club's founding and the Masters Tournament.

Magnolia Lane

Row of sixty-one magnolia trees that line the entrance to the Augusta National clubhouse from Washington Road. The trees were planted just prior to the Civil War by the Berckmans family who founded Fruitlands Nurseries.

Founders' Circle

Upon entering the club from Washington Road, golfers make their way along Magnolia Lane, passing sixty-one trees planted by the Berckmans family in the mid-1800s. At the end of Magnolia Lane the Founders' Circle is situated at the base of the flagpole, just in back of the flower bed that rings the outline of the Augusta National logo. Plaques situated there are dedicated to club cofounders Bobby Jones and Clifford Roberts.

Ike's Pond

Ike's Pond occupies three acres immediately in back of the Eisenhower Cabin. Like the cabin, the pond is also named in honor of Dwight D. Eisenhower. Two holes added to the Augusta National's Par-3 Course by Tom Fazio in 1986 play over Ike's Pond.

Par-3 Course

Constructed in 1958 by architect George Cobb, with help from Clifford Roberts, the course was expanded to eleven holes in 1986 by Tom Fazio. The new holes provide a picturesque backdrop for the final two holes of the annual Par-3 Contest staged on Wednesday of Masters Week.

A fountain commemorating the Par-3 Contest winners dating back to Sam Snead's inaugural win in 1960 is located opposite the course's Number 1 tee box. No golfer has ever won the Par-3 event at midweek and gone on to win the Masters Tournament. In 1990 Raymond Floyd came closest to accomplishing the feat when he won the Par-3 contest and later that week lost in a playoff to Nick Faldo in the main event.

The Hogan Bridge

Spanning Rae's Creek between the eleventh and twelfth greens in Amen Corner, the bridge is dedicated to Ben Hogan's efforts in 1953 in establishing the then single-round scoring mark of 274. The dedication ceremony took place on April 2, 1958. The two-time champion's record stood until 1965 when Jack Nicklaus scored 17-under-par 271 en route to his second Masters win, a scoring mark equaled by Raymond Floyd in 1976. The benchmark was reestablished by Tiger Woods at 18-under-par 270 en route to his first Masters victory in 1997.

The Nelson Bridge

The bridge, dedicated at the same time as the Hogan Bridge, connects golfers from the thirteenth tee to the fairway of this par-5 hole and commemorates Byron Nelson's comeback win in the 1937 Masters. Nelson played Amen Corner to perfection, scoring 2-3 over the twelfth and thirteenth holes to gain six shots

First Week In April circa 2001 The Crow's Nest atop the Augusta National Clubhouse overlooks the golf course and tables with umbrellas reserved for guests of the club.

Serving print and electronic media from around the world, the new Media Center was opened in 1990 to replace the old Quonset hut erected in 1953.

on leader Ralph Guldahl and win the tournament by two shots.

The Sarazen Bridge

Located at the fifteenth green, this bridge honors Gene Sarazen's final round double-eagle, the celebrated "shot heard round the world", en route to winning the 1935 Augusta National Invitation Tournament. Bobby Jones was one of only a dozen or so witnesses to the feat, which brought the Tournament to the forefront of the national news. The bridge was dedicated in 1955.

Press Building

Serving print and electronic media from around the world, the new Media Center was opened in 1990 to replace the old Quonset hut erected in 1953. The inside lounge area is dedicated to Charles Bartlett, the long-time *Chicago Tribune* golf editor who was also instrumental in helping found the Golf Writers Association of America. The lounge was dedicated during Masters Week 1968, five months after Bartlett's death.

Record Fountain

Situated to the left of the Number 17 green is a hexagonal water fountain bearing the names of Masters champions and their respective scores. Dedicated for the twenty-fifth Anniversary Masters Tournament in 1959, the fountain also includes the progression of records established at the Augusta National Golf Club.

Arnold Palmer Plaque

Located on a water fountain in back of the Number 16 tee is a plaque commemorating Arnold Palmer's contributions, including four Masters Tournament victories that occurred every other year beginning with 1958 (1958, '60, '62, and '64). The plaque was dedicated in 1995, and Palmer competed in his fiftieth consecutive and final Masters Tournament in 2004.

Jack Nicklaus Plaque

Attached to a water fountain between the sixteenth and seventeenth holes, the Jack Nicklaus Plaque honors the Masters Tournaments only six-time champion (1963, '65, '66, '72, '75, and '86) who won his last title at age forty-six. The plaque was dedicated during Masters Week 1998.

Eisenhower Tree

The loblolly pine in the left-center fairway of the seventeenth hole is named for former president and club member Dwight D. Eisenhower. A constant source

Clubhouse, circa 1934 Back of Berckmans residence and Fruitlands Nurseries offices next door. (Photo by Tony Sheehan. Courtesy of Joseph M. Lee III.)

of frustration to Ike during his many rounds of golf at the Augusta National in the 1950s, he proposed the tree be removed.

Rae's Creek

The creek running between the eleventh and twelfth greens is named for John Rae, whose eighteenth-century home was reportedly the farthest outpost up the Savannah River from Fort Augusta. A tributary of Rae's Creek winds its way along the thirteenth fairway and fronts the thirteenth green.

Masters single-round scoring co-medallist Nick Price reportedly once questioned the word "Amen" affixed to the corner because it was there, he reasoned, that he just began to pray.

Amen Corner

This name was first used in an article by Herbert Warren Wind in *Sports Illustrated* in 1958 to denote the eleventh, twelfth, and thirteenth holes. Arnold Palmer won his first Masters Tournament that year after a favorable ruling upheld his free drop of a plugged ball at Number 12. Masters single-round scoring co-medallist Nick Price (63 on Saturday, 1986, tied by Greg Norman in 1996) reportedly once questioned the word "Amen" affixed to the corner because it was there, he reasoned, that he just began to pray.

Privet Hedge

Shortly after the Fruitlands Nurseries corporation was formed in 1858, ten privet hedges from France were imported to the grounds. The prominent hedges displayed throughout the grounds of the Augusta National Golf Club are the outgrowth of those few plants.

Clubhouse

The first cement structure in the south, the majestic clubhouse was built by Dennis Redmond in 1854. The structure was slated to be torn down in 1926 and replaced with a high-rise resort hotel.

Ike's Tree The large pine in the left center of the fairway is named after former president Dwight D. Eisenhower. (© Historic Golf Photos–Ron Watts Collection.)

Building Bridges Byron Nelson and Ben Hogan stand alongside Bobby Jones and Clifford Roberts (in golf cart) during the 1958 dedication ceremonies for the Hogan and Nelson Bridges. (© Historic Golf Photos–Ron Watts Collection.)

Sarazen Scene circa 1955 Masters Tournament patrons attend dedication ceremonies for the Gene Sarazen Bridge at the 15th hole of the Augusta

The clubhouse features the Trophy Room and Champions Locker Room on the second floor; and a third floor that includes the "Crow's Nest."

Crow's Nest

On the third floor of the clubhouse is a thirty-by-forty foot room that houses four cubicles. The space accommodates amateur invitees during the week of the Masters Tournament. The top of the room features an eleven-by-eleven foot cupola called the "Crow's Nest," a four-sided viewing area that can be accessed only by ladder.

Big Oak Tree

Located directly in back of the clubhouse, the "Big Oak Tree" has been a traditional gathering spot for media interviews with players following their rounds. The tree was planted shortly after the Berckmans residence (Augusta National Clubhouse) was constructed in 1854. The lawn adjacent to the oak tree is reserved for members and guests who are free to lounge at tables with umbrellas.

Augusta National Golf Club Cabins

Ten cabins for members and guests ring the Par-3 Course at the Augusta National Golf Club. The three most visible of the structures are the Eisenhower, Butler, and Roberts Cabins. Constructed in 1953, the Eisenhower Cabin housed President and Mrs. Dwight D. Eisenhower during stays at the Augusta National. The Butler Cabin is home to the CBS broadcast studio during Masters Week.

Located directly in back of the clubhouse, the "Big Oak Tree" has been a traditional gathering spot for media interviews with players following their rounds.

Augusta National Golf Club, circa 1953 Early aerial photograph of the Augusta National clubhouse and nearby cottages. (© Historic Golf Photos–Ron Watts Collection.)

Bridging the Gap The Ben Hogan Bridge spans Rae's Creek at the twelfth green with the Byron Nelson Bridge from the thirteenth tee in the background. (© Historic Golf Photos–Ron Watts Collection.)

MacKenzie Magic—Principles at Play in Augusta

MacKenzie's thirteen principles were first published as a series of articles on course design in the early 1900s and represent a sampling of his brilliance on the subject. The guidelines were later published in 1920 in MacKenzie's book *Golf Architecture*, which was still more than a decade prior to his work with Bobby Jones at the Augusta National Golf Club. MacKenzie reiterated the principles in his second book, *The Spirit of St. Andrews*, compiled shortly after the Augusta National was constructed, but the manuscript was not published until 1995 when it was uncovered. In a complete show of confidence in his original work, MacKenzie made no changes to his thirteen general principles in the two decades between when the books were penned.

Following are MacKenzie's thirteen general principles for course design, along with excerpts from his works and commentary on how these relate to the Augusta National Golf Club.

1 The course, where possible, should be arranged in two loops of nine holes.

"During recent years in the United States I have had more sleepless nights owing to committees being obsessed by this principle than anything else, and I have often regretted that it had ever been propounded. If land for a golf course lends itself readily to constructing the two loops, well and good, but it is a great mistake to sacrifice excellent natural features for the purpose of obtaining it."
—Alister MacKenzie

Owing to MacKenzie's first principle, the Augusta National Golf Club features two sets of nine holes that loop back toward the clubhouse and to the inside of the starting holes on each nine. At the same time, the layout affords an abundance of space for spectators to congregate in the center of the design. Tee boxes for the first and tenth hole and greens for the ninth and eighteenth holes are situated within yards of each other to form a semicircle around the practice putting area within a few yards of the clubhouse. This layout affords an abundance of spectator viewing sites within a compact area. While the concept works extremely well at the Augusta National, MacKenzie was quick to point out that the best land on a golf course not be compromised to make this principle work.

2 There should be a large proportion of good two-shot holes, two or three drive-and-pitch holes, and at least four one-shot holes.

"It is true that there are certain general considerations which should influence us in routing a course. It is an advantage to start off with three or four one-shot holes to get people away. It is also advisable to arrange the short holes so that there will be a rest after playing one or more of the long ones.

"I usually like to have four one-shot holes, two in each half, but on occasion we have had as small a number as two or perhaps three, and on other occasions as many as five or six. We should be influenced primarily by the nature of the ground and what is going to give the best test of golf and most lasting pleasure to the greatest number.

"It is generally acknowledged that a golf course should finish with three or four long holes. The advantage of this is that the player who is two or three down still has a chance of squaring or winning his match, and it frequently results in the interest of the match being sustained right up to the end. This is a point, however, on which one must not be too dogmatic. The nature of the ground may not lend itself to four long holes." —Alister MacKenzie

With a dozen par 4s, four par 3s and 5s (equally distributed among each nine), the Augusta National again fits MacKenzie's plan as a well-balanced layout. MacKenzie concentrated on a course layout that would play to "equal 4s" (par 72) and left it to Jones to affix the actual par values to each hole. While technology and course changes have altered the dynamics of the seventh hole, MacKenzie's favorite hole layout, Number 3, remains a showcase of the drive-and-pitch.

The Augusta National does not close with "three or four long holes in a row," but represents a perfect example of MacKenzie relaxing a rule in favor of a far superior utilization of the overall landscape. As a result, one could hardly imagine a more demanding closing nine holes in golf history. The back nine includes two of the most difficult holes (tenth and twelfth) in Masters history and the testy eleventh that has determined more Masters sudden death playoffs than any other. Following are two par 5s over water (thirteenth and fifteenth), a hole sans sand (fourteenth) that features treacherous mounds instead, the par-3 sixteenth over water, the putting intensive seventeenth, and the long, uphill strategic test at eighteenth. Withstand the back nine in Augusta and a green jacket awaits.

The front side closes with two long, demanding holes (par-5 eighth and par-4 ninth) that feature dramatic elevation changes and likely played a factor in the reversal of the nines while MacKenzie and Jones first laid out the course.

3 There should be little walking between the greens and tees, and the course should be arranged so that in the first instance there is always a slight walk forwards from the green to the next tee; then the holes are sufficiently elastic to be lengthened in the future if necessary.

"There is, for example, the question of the length of the course, length of holes and details similar to these, but they are of minor importance compared with the main object of making the course interesting. Designers of golf courses have laid down the law as to the total length of the course, the exact number of one-shot, two-shot and three-shot holes and even the sequence of these holes in the round. How often I have seen a golf course ruined in the attempt to extend it to what is generally considered championship length.

"Some of the committees who choose the courses for championships are responsible for this. They are obsessed with length and allow it to outweigh much more important considerations. It would be possible to make a golf course measuring 5,000 yards a much finer test of golf than some of those approaching 7,000 yards on which championships have been played." —Alister MacKenzie

The visionary in MacKenzie begins to peek through in this principle. Due to the impact of technology on the game, the Augusta National Golf Club accommodated nicely the addition of nearly 300 yards in length and major changes to nine holes prior to the 2002 Masters. Meanwhile, the time spent moving from putting surface to the next tee is minimal at all hole locations. Bobby Jones was equally interested in providing spectators with an abundance of viewing opportunities during the course of a single round, and his views on the subject are included in the Augusta National's Spectator Guide published each spring.

4 The greens and fairways should be sufficiently undulating, but there should be no hill climbing.

"In regard to the fourth principle, it used to be a common fallacy that greens were to be made dead flat. Even on some of the best courses at the present day you find a reaction lately against undulating greens, but this, I believe, is entirely due to the fact that the undulations have little humps or of the "ridge and furrow" type. Natural undulations are the exact opposite of the artificial ridge and furrow. The latter has a narrow hollow and a broad ridge, whereas the former has a large, bold sweeping hollow and a narrow ridge.

"In constructing natural looking undulations, one should attempt to study the manner in which those among sand dunes are formed. These are fashioned by the wind blowing up the sand in the form of waves which have become gradually turfed over in the course of time. Natural undulations are therefore of a similar shape to the waves one sees by the seashore and are of all shapes and sizes, but are characterized by the fact that the hollows between the waves are broader than the waves themselves. If undulations are made like this there are always plenty of comparatively flat places where the greenkeeper can put the flag, and there should never be any necessity to cut a hole in the slope.

"A test of a good undulation is that it should be easy to use a mowing machine over it. If undulations are made of the kind I describe, it is hardly possible to make them too bold or too large. Perhaps the most irritating type of undulation is the finicky little hump or side slope which you do not see until after you have missed your putt and then begin to wonder why it has not gone into the hole.

"An almost equally common delusion is that fairways should be flat. I quite agree that there is nothing worse than a fairway on a severe side slope, but on the other hand, there are few things more monotonous than playing every shot from a dead flat fairway. All the British Championship courses owe their interest to their undulations."
—Alister MacKenzie

A common viewpoint in the early 1900s was that fairways and putting surfaces should be flat, but MacKenzie felt that perspective was promoted due to poorly constructed undulations. He viewed the undulations as an integral part of a golf course's personality. "Only when one studied the formation of wind-swept sand dunes along the seashore," MacKenzie concluded, "could they comprehend the concept of a natural looking undulation." The challenge was to draw upon the vastly superior links courses of the day and emulate these inland. MacKenzie's simple but ultimate test for what he termed "natural looking undulations" was that it be easy to utilize a mower over.

When it comes to MacKenzie's layout at the Augusta National Golf Club, the countless undulations remain both the beauty and key to the course's design. Hill climbing being a more subjective term, it is safe to say that a week's worth of walking the layout provides a challenge even to those in the best of shape, especially if the week happens to bring a not uncommon spike in temperature. More importantly, MacKenzie stressed the avoidance of severe side slopes in fairways, of which the Augusta National has none. Winner of an unprecedented six green jackets over the span of twenty-eight years, Jack Nicklaus has aptly described the Augusta National as a "young man's" course.

5 Every hole should have a different character.

"In regard to the fifth principle—that every hole should have a different character—a common mistake is to follow prevailing fashions.

"The great thing in constructing a golf course is to ensure variety and make everything look natural. The greatest compliment that can be paid to a constructor is for players to think his artificial work is natural.

"I always attempt not only to make every hole different on a golf course, but never conspicuously reproduce two exactly similar holes. I attempt to get inspirations by seizing on any natural features and accentuating the best golfing points on them." —Alister MacKenzie

No two consecutive holes at the Augusta National are laid out in the same direction, and no two holes in succession on the front nine are affixed the same par values. In addition, MacKenzie was not one to follow the fashion of the day. His utilization of aesthetic and cost-effective mounds instead of bunkers was considered revolutionary. To his credit, each hole at the Augusta National provides a different feel, challenge, and risk-reward factor unique to each hole. The layout remains a model of design-work that showcases an ever changing landscape and forces golfers to showcase a different element of their games on each succeeding hole.

6 There should be a minimum of blindness for the approach shots.

"A blind tee shot may be forgiven, or a full shot to the green on a seaside course, when the greens can usually be located accurately by the position of the surrounding hummocks, but an approach shot should never be blind, as this prevents an expert player, except by a fluke, from placing his approach so near the hole that he gets down in one putt.
"On a seaside course there may be a certain amount of pleasurable excitement in running up to the top of a hillock in the hope of seeing your ball near the flag, but this is a kind of thing of which one gets rather tired as one grows older." —Alister MacKenzie

The approach to the seventh green, which was rebuilt by associate Perry Maxwell in 1937, is the most glaring exception to this guiding MacKenzie principle. MacKenzie designed the original seventh to be played as a pitch-and-run to the green. Aided by advancements in technology, golfers began hitting drives close to the putting surface. At the suggestion of two-time Masters champion Horton Smith, the seventh green was reconstructed. The result is a blind, uphill approach to a putting surface guarded by bunkers from all sides. While the flag at the top of the pin is fully visible on approach, it is a situation MacKenzie would likely have avoided.

7 The course should have beautiful surroundings, and all the artificial features should have so natural an appearance that a stranger is unable to distinguish them from nature itself.

"Another erroneous idea which is prevalent is that beauty does not matter on a golf course. One often hears players say they "don't care a tinker's cuss" about their surroundings, what they want is good golf. One of the best known writers on golf has been jeering at architects for attempting to make beautiful bunkers. If he prefers ugly bunkers, ugly greens, and ugly surroundings generally, he is welcome them, but I do not think for an instant that he believes what he is writing about, for at the same time he talks about the beauties of the natural courses. The chief object of every golf architect or greenkeeper worth his salt is to imitate the beauties of nature so closely as to make his work indistinguishable from Nature herself." —Alister MacKenzie

Whether one plays golf or not, a walk through the springtime setting in Augusta, with its dogwoods and azaleas in bloom and impeccably manicured grounds, makes for a breathtaking and unforgettable journey. One of MacKenzie's tests for an artificial hazard was that it be in plain view from the tee, but unseen when looking back from the putting surface. MacKenzie's was a wide open layout with hazards placed sparingly for their individual strategic values and never to penalize a golfer. It is ironic that the cosmetic bunker in the tenth fairway, by far the largest on the course, is named for MacKenzie, who disdained such artificial areas lacking strategic importance.

8 There should be a sufficient number of heroic carries from the tee, but the course should be arranged so that the weaker player with the loss of a stroke or portion of a stroke shall always have an alternative route open to him.

"The majority of golfers are agreed, I think, that an ideal hole should be a difficult one. It is true there are some who would have it difficult for everyone but themselves… It is the successful negotiation of difficulties, or apparent ones, which gives rise to pleasurable excitement and makes a hole interesting." —Alister MacKenzie

MacKenzie played upon what he termed "the spirit of adventure" in attempting to challenge golfers on his courses. Drawing from MacKenzie's experience in designing Cypress Point, Jones hit countless golf balls at the design to best determine its "heroic carries" and the degree of difficulty golfers of all skill levels would face. The result is that the Augusta National is the hallmark of "heroic carries."

9 There should be infinite variety in the strokes required to play the various holes—viz., interesting brassy shots, iron shots, pitch and run-up shots.

"There are many leading players who condemn the strategy aspect of golf. They only see one line to the hole, and that is usually the direct one. They cannot see why they should, as in dog-legged holes, be ever compelled to play to one or other side of the direct line . . . . Why should not even an open champion occasionally have a shot that the long handicap man is frequently required to play?

"At the risk of being boresome I have given a considerable amount of space to emphasizing the importance of creating variety in approach shots, as I feel that progress in golf architecture is dependant on creating courses of this description." —Alister MacKenzie

The *New York Times* of January 17, 1933, carried an article that featured remarks about the new Augusta National Golf Club from USGA Vice President John G. Jackson and Treasurer Archie M. Reid, and "According to both golf officials, the greens are varying in shape and demand an unusual variety of approach shots."

Despite advances in technology, the Augusta National requires a full range of shot-making skills in determining its Masters champion. Lengthened to 7,270 yards prior to the 2002 tournament, the Augusta National expects golfers to utilize the same "maximum of mental labor" that MacKenzie used in devising the layout.

10 There should be a complete absence of the annoyance and irritation caused by the necessity of searching for lost balls.

"Most golfers have an erroneous view of the real object of hazards. The majority of them simply look upon a hazard as a means of punishing a bad shot, whereas their real object is to make the game more interesting.

"Being a Scotsman, I am naturally opposed to water in its undiluted state. I am also opposed to a hazard involving the risk of a lost ball… On the other hand, I am very much in favor of utilizing water where it exists as a natural feature, particularly if there is a clean bottom and there is a chance of recovering one's ball." —Alister MacKenzie

During a late-1980s practice round, Lee Trevino was spotted fishing golf balls out of Rae's Creek at the twelfth hole. When questioned by the media afterward about his treasure hunt he replied that the objects of his affection were worth money. The Masters would prove the lone major that Trevino would not cash in on, and he felt MacKenzie's layout favored the long hitter. But in 1989, at age forty-nine, when Trevino posted 67 in the opening round, he became the oldest player ever to lead the Masters tournament. He did not lose any golf balls that day.

11 The course should be so interesting that even the plus man is constantly stimulated to improve his game in attempting shots he has hitherto been unable to play.

"A golf course which merely caters for an everlasting pitch at every hole can never be entirely satisfactory. Any player under a sixteen handicap can play a pitch shot, but few of even the best players can play a run up shot. Bobby Jones never appreciated the Old Course at St. Andrews until he had learned to play this shot.

"Narrow fairways bordered by long grass make bad golfers. They do so by destroying the harmony and continuity of the game and causing a stilted and a cramped style, destroying all freedom of play." —Alister MacKenzie

MacKenzie and Jones did not take a design step without first considering the ultimate effect it would have on the average golfer. When they designed the Augusta National Golf Club in 1931 they did not have the Masters Tournament specifically in mind, but rather a layout that would bring pleasure to the most golfers and stand as a challenge for every skill level.

MacKenzie also favored no more than two bunkers per hole and felt that many courses overused the hazards. Still, the Augusta National employed far fewer bunkers than any of his other layouts. Likely as much a cost-cutting measure as for strategic value, thirty-six bunkers sketched into the original design were later scaled back to twenty-two. The Augusta National Golf Club now includes forty-four bunkers over seventeen holes.

When the Augusta National officially opened in January 1933, its twenty-two bunkers were hailed as a revolutionary design concept. Until that point in golf history, it was more popular to penalize golfers than strategize courses and more likely to see twenty-two hazards on one hole alone.

12 The course should be so arranged that the long handicap player, or even the absolute beginner, should be able to enjoy his round in spite of the fact that he is piling up a big score.

"One of the objects in placing hazards is to give the players as much pleasurable excitement as possible. On many inland courses there is not a thrill on the whole round, and yet on some of the British Championship courses one rarely takes a club out of the bag without having an interesting shot to play.

"There are some leading players who honestly dislike the dramatic element in golf. They hate anything which is likely to interfere with a constant succession of threes and fours. They look at everything in the 'card and pencil spirit.'

"The average club member on the other hand is a keen sportsman who looks upon golf in the 'spirit of adventure,' and that is why St. Andrews and courses modeled on similar ideals appeals to him." —Alister MacKenzie

That at least one of MacKenzie's thirteen rules is dedicated to the high-handicap golfer confirmed his early commitment to designs that would accommodate the widest range of talent. One need only peek in on the week set aside at the end of the season, when local officials, employees, and media are invited to play the Augusta National, to see this guiding principle of MacKenzie's in action. As MacKenzie and Jones intended, the course remains a challenge to competitive golfers and a source of enjoyment for those of lesser skill.

Following the grand opening of the Augusta National in January 1933, the *New York Times* reported, "Not only were the low handicap players enthusiastic over the course, but so were the 'duffers' of the party who were in the majority. For them not only the scarcity of traps but the presence, on all the long holes, of "alternate" routes were outstanding good points."

13 The course should be equally good during winter and summer, the texture of the greens and fairways should be perfect, and the approaches should have the same consistency as the greens.

"The common mistake is not to mow greens during the winter months. I have not the slightest doubt that mowing greens during the winter months is beneficial to them: it keeps the grass from becoming coarse." —Alister MacKenzie

Following the course's grand opening in January 1933, the *New York Times* noted that USGA Treasurer Archie M. Reid was impressed with the texture of the fairways at the Augusta National. "Bobby's done a marvelous thing there, using Bermuda grass as a base and Italian Rye to soften and give color." In 1983, the transition was made from bermuda to bent grass on its putting surfaces.

The Augusta National Golf Club is open to play for members and guests from October through the following Memorial Day weekend. Its fairways and putting surfaces are maintained as impeccably during the season as for the Masters Tournament staged annually in April.

Additional MacKenzie Design Philosophies

"On many courses there are far too many bunkers. The sides of the fairways are riddled with them, and many of the courses would be equally interesting and infinitely more pleasurable if half the bunkers were turfed over and converted into grassy hollows. It is often possible to make a hole sufficiently interesting with one or two bunkers at the most."

"A bunker eating into a green is by far the most equitable way of giving a golfer full advantage for accurate play. It not only penalizes the man who is in it but also everyone who is wide of it."

"As a rule, hazards are placed too far away from the green they are intended to guard. They should be placed immediately on the edge of the green and then, particularly if they are in the form of smooth hillocks and hollows, the player who is wide of them has an extremely difficult pitch and is frequently worse off than the man who is among them."

"Most of the best inland courses owe their popularity to the grouping of trees. Groups of trees are the most effective way of preventing players reaching the green with their second shots after playing their drives in the wrong direction. No bunkers guarding the green seem to be able to prevent them doing so."

"Many green committees ruin one's handiwork by planting trees like rows of soldiers along the borders of the fairways. Alternatively, groups of trees, planted irregularly, create most fascinating golf, and give players many opportunities of showing their skill and judgment in slicing, pulling round, or attempting to loft over them. Some of the most spectacular shots I have ever seen have been around, over or through narrow gaps in trees."

"A hazard placed in the exact position where a player would naturally go is frequently the most interesting situation, as a special effort is then needed to get over it or avoid it."

Bibliography

2000 Masters Journal. Augusta, Ga.: Augusta National Golf Club, 2000.

2001 Masters Journal. Augusta, Ga.: Augusta National Golf Club, 2001.

2002 Masters Journal. Augusta, Ga.: Augusta National Golf Club, 2002.

2002 Masters Media Guide, April 8–14. Augusta, Ga.: Augusta National, Inc., 2002.

2003 Masters Journal. Augusta, Ga.: Augusta National Golf Club, 2003.

2004 Masters Media Guide, April 5–11. Augusta, Ga.: Augusta National, Inc., 2004.

2005 Masters Media Guide, April 7–10. Augusta, Ga.: Augusta National, Inc., 2004.

"Augusta Archives–Online Archives," Morris Communications, http://www.augustaarchives.com.

"Bobby Jones," Jonesheirs, Inc., www.bobbyjones.com.

Buchen, Terry. "MacKenzie's Mysterious Manuscript." *Golf Course News,* March 1995.

Cashin, Edward J. *The Story of Augusta.* Spartanburg, S.C.: The Reprint Company, 1996.

Christian, Frank. *Augusta National and the Masters.* Chelsea, Mich.: Sleeping Bear Press, 1996.

Clayton, Ward. *Men on the Bag: The Caddies of Augusta National.* Ann Arbor, Mich.: Sports Media Group, 2004.

DeBoer-Langworthy, Carol. "The Boer War." http://www.modjourn.brown.edu/mjp/Essays/Boer.html.

Doak, Tom, Dr. James Scott, and Raymund Haddock. *The Life and Work of Dr. Alister Mackenzie.* Chelsea, Mich.: Sleeping Bear Press, 2001.

"Golf Links to the Past," www.golflinkstothepast.com.

Jones, Bobby. "Golf Is My Game," 1959, as reprinted in the *2002 Masters Journal.*

Kerrville, (TX) Daily times, Byron Nelson Remembers Joe Finger, September 30, 2003 http://web.dailytimes.com/story.lasso?wcd=7503

Lewis, Catherine M. *Considerable Passions: Golf, The Masters, and the Legacy of Bobby Jones.* Chicago: Triumph Books, 2000.

Lucas, George L., III. *Augusta National Yardage Book.* 2003 Revision.

MacKenzie, Alister, Dr., *Golf Architecture*, 1920, Simpkin, Marshall, Hamilton, Kent and Co. Reprinted 1987, Ailsa, Inc.

MacKenzie, Alister, with Foreword by Robert Tyre Jones Jr. *The Spirit of St. Andrews.* New York: Broadway Books, ____.

"Official Site of the Masters Golf Tournament," Augusta National, Inc., http://www.masters.org.

Owen, David. *The Making of the Masters.* New York: Simon and Schuster, 2003.

"PGA Tour," PGA Tour, Inc., http://www.golfweb.com.

Price, Charles. *A Golf Story.* Chicago: Triumph Books, 2001.

Richardson, William D., "A Golf Course for the Forgotten Man," *New York Times*, August 7, 1932.

Roberts, Clifford. *The Story of the Augusta National Golf Club.* Garden City, N.Y.: Doubleday, 1976.

"The Ryder Cup Official Website," The PGA of America, Ryder Cup Ltd., and Turner Sports Interactive, http:www.pga.com/rydercup/.

Shackelford, Geoff. "Hidden Hazards," *Masters Journal 2003.* Augusta: Augusta National, Inc., 2003.

Sowell, David. *The Masters.* Washington, D.C.: Brassey's, Inc., 2003.

Spectator Guide, Augusta National Golf Club, April 7–13, 2003. Augusta, Ga.: Augusta National, Inc., 2003.

Whitten, Ron. "Augusta: It's a Work in Progress," *Golf Digest.* April 2000.

WJBF-TV (Masters Reports Interviews)

Yocom, Guy. "Clash of the Titans," *2000 Masters Journal.* Augusta, Ga.: Augusta National Golf Club, 2000.

Special Thanks

To professional golfer, sketch artist, and friend William Lanier III, whose artwork brings Alister MacKenzie's original designs to life.

To Ward Clayton, Director of Editorial Services for the PGA Tour, who takes up residence at my home each Masters Week and whose love of golf and knowledge of Augusta have been invaluable sources of information and inspiration.

To Glenn Greenspan, Director of Communications, Augusta National Golf Club, and associate Jill Maxwell for their aid in providing key information in support of this project.

To Bill Baab, *Augusta Chronicle* outdoor sportswriter and historian, whose continued support and editorial services bar none are deeply appreciated.

To Joseph M. Lee III and his dedication to furthering Augusta's rich history. It is courtesy of Mr. Lee that Tony Sheehan's early photos of Alister MacKenzie's design at the Augusta National Golf Club are available for presentation in this book.

To Buddy Dickson and Pat Turner at Augusta's Summerville Photo for use of special photos of the late George Schaeffer that bring us a closer look at MacKenzie's later design from many intriguing angles.

To Michael O'Byrne for use of photographs of the Augusta National Golf Course, circa 1994.

To Dr. Joe Dromsky for use of his personal collection of photographs.

To the Western Golf Association for use of photos from early Masters Tournaments.

To Milledge Murray, Frank Christian, Allen Riddick, Steve Leone, Tom Moore, Forest Hills Golf Club, Palmetto Golf Club, and the Augusta Museum of History for additional artwork and information.

To the hardworking staff at Ann Arbor Media Group; to Skip DeWall for his vision, to Lynne Johnson and Carol Bokas for their day-to-day efforts in keeping the project on track.